HOPE
IN A
BROKEN
WORLD

*Five Principles of F.A.I.T.H. Not Only When You
Endure Various Trials but How to Persevere and
Rejoice in the Midst of Them*

Joe B. Lamphere

ISBN 978-1-63844-633-0 (paperback)
ISBN 978-1-63844-634-7 (digital)

Christian Faith Publishing, Inc.
832 Park Avenue
Meadville, PA 16335
www.christianfaithpublishing.com

Printed in the United States of America

Contents

Introduction

Life in a broken world is complicated, and certain to be full of the unexpected. Where do we turn to help us answer life's tough questions? We live in a time when everything's in crisis. For instance, the outbreak of the Coronavirus disease (COVID–19) has now spread to over 220 countries around the globe. We see a suffering world with real human heartache wailing and mourning the tragic death of our loved ones from everywhere. Many of us have been experiencing a high level of anxiety and hardship, fearful of the unknown, and having thoughts of uncertainty and feelings of hopelessness.

Then, the news, we see a troubling case in Minneapolis when a White police officer took the life of a Black man. Thousands of protestors and rioters flocked to the streets of major cities all across the US. Violence and lawlessness soon followed, and footage was all caught on camera for the viewing public. ABC, Fox News, CBS, NBC, CNN, and MSNBC evening newscasts provided an aerial view of the chaos happening on the ground. In the moment, it was like watching sheep with no shepherd. If ever there were a need for a shepherd, it is when there is injustice in the world.

Another unsettling and astonishing event was the case in Washington DC, when a mob of protestor's and extremists, on a pursuit for change, breached the US Capitol, entered the house chamber, and where a woman was tragically shot by a Capitol police officer trying to scale through a broken window frame. She and at least four others tragically lost their lives.

How wonderful it would be to live in a world without war, health epidemics, disease, crime, addictions, hostility, or injustice. Sometimes, we may never know why things happen. Circumstances and events aren't always possible to understand with our sense of justice. On these sad days of events, it reminded me of Charles Swindoll's well-regarded psalm about attitude, concluding with this statement, "I am convinced that life is 10 percent what happens to me and 90 percent how I react to it." How do you respond when things don't turn out according to your plan? The truth is things may seem to be out of our control, but they're not out of God's control.

By nature, we don't like taking orders—they mess with our self-reliance and pursuit of happiness. Christians, however, are called to live differently from the norm. We are called to follow God's commands. And as we do so, God helps us discover the happiness we have longed for. The most famous commands are the Ten Commandments, which God gave to the Israelites thousands of years ago. The commandment "You shall have no other gods before me" (Exodus 20:3 New International Version) means that we are not to honor anything above God—be it a house, job, spouse, money, sex, power, social media sites, politics, country, president or our own selfish ambition or pleasure. God gave the Israelites other commandments to help them know how to relate to Him and to other people.

As Christians, we become worldly when we love the world's ways more than we love God's way. Adopting any of the evil perspectives and norms of the "prince of this world" (Satan) is worldly. He deceives and tricks people for his own greedy satisfaction. His ways run contrary to those of God's. The truth is, when we accept worldly values and patterns, we become programmed to the kind of crafty thinking and living that has no place in heaven. The Bible says, "Don't become so well-adjusted to your culture that you fit into it without even thinking. Instead, fix your attention on God. You'll be changed from the inside out. Readily recognize what he wants from you, and quickly respond to it. Unlike the culture around you, always dragging you down to its level of immaturity, God brings the best out of you, develops well-formed maturity in you" (Romans 12:2 The Message Bible).

God knows what will give us the best life here as well as the best life after we die. God either causes or allows certain things to happen. He allows good to result from the evil that others intend. He causes people to move contrary to natural inclinations and to promote His cause. Therefore, "Do not be afraid or discouraged, for the Lord will personally go ahead of you. He will be with you; He will neither fail you nor abandon you" (Deuteronomy 31:8 New Living Translation).

Christians need the rigorous training and instruction that comes from the study of God's Word in order to navigate a hostile world and overcome worldly desires. Jesus himself said, "I have told you all this so that you may have peace in Me. Here on earth you will have many trials and sorrows. But take heart, because I have overcome the world" (John 16:33 NLT). Although we are taught to enjoy the things of this world, our goal is to have our hearts and minds focused on things above. Do you think that's even possible considering we're living in a world that seems to be getting progressively out of balance?

The world, Satan, and our human nature put many obstacles in our paths that can cause us to lose our footing. We encounter even more of these stumbling blocks when we leave the path that God has laid out for us in His Word. Here's some encouraging news: "For every child of God defeats this evil world, and we achieve this victory through our faith. And who can win this battle against the world? Only those who believe that Jesus is the Son of God" (1 John 5:4–5 NLT). Without faith it is impossible to please God.

What is faith? "Now faith is confidence in what we hope for and assurance about what we do not see" (Hebrews 11:1 NIV). Saving faith is not something we are born with; it's something we receive in a flash of light the moment we first believe in Christ. The Bible says, "For it is by grace you have been saved, through faith—and this is not from yourselves, it is the gift of God" (Ephesians 2:8 NIV). The true shepherd irresistibly pursues His people in spite of our rejection of Him to reconcile the broken relationship and give us life.

Our Hope in a broken world is anchored in the very life of Christ.

Regardless if various trials or circumstances go away or not; triumphantly, we can rejoice—right in the midst of affliction. "Being confident in this, that He who began a good work in you will carry it on to completion until the day of Christ Jesus" (Philippians 1:6 NIV). We are not the ones holding onto God; He is the One holding onto us. And nothing can snatch you away from that truth. God is in absolute control. What God starts He finishes. He is faithful and trustworthy; His unfailing love and goodness endures forever. God has a plan to reach the world and it's through You! The Bible says, "Such things were written in the Scriptures long ago to teach us. And the Scriptures give us hope and encouragement as we wait patiently for God's promises to be fulfilled" (Romans 15:4 NLT). Although we cannot see this promised future, we know that it will one day happen. Therefore, our hope of a future through Him is certain.

In this book, you'll learn inspirational stories in the Old Testament and the New Testament that have been preserved for us as examples of faith as a response to suffering, injustice, and difficulty. The good news is that the Bible shows how the "faith challenges" of those who lived so long ago can shape our character and help us get to know the Lord better in our lives today. In this book, you'll learn five principles of faith not only when you endure trials of many kinds but also how to persevere and rejoice in the midst of them.

Much of the insight here comes from multiple translations of Scripture intended to increase your level of understanding along with teachings from the NIV Starting Point Study Bible to help you cultivate heart-to-heart intimacy with God. The Bible is alive with God's spirit and it helps us understand God's love and to show us how were supposed to live in a broken world. My hope is that as you read, study, and apply God's Word it will penetrate your heart and transform your life—like it has mine.

PRINCIPLE 1

Follow God as the Leader

Trust in the Lord with all your heart and lean not
on your own understanding; in all your ways submit
to him, and he will make your paths straight.
—Proverbs 3:5–6 (NIV)

If you were going to start a worldwide movement, who would you pick to be on your board of directors and promote your views? A team of the best and the brightest, the economically wealthy, powerful lawmakers, media personalities, and social influencers? That's not whom Jesus Christ chose. At least four of the men He chose to follow and learn from Him were fishermen. These men weren't people who could sway the masses with their rhetoric and sophistication. But they were committed to following Jesus, and His power working through them enabled them to win thousands to faith in Him.

Jesus told Simon (later called Peter) and his brother, Andrew, "Come, follow me and I will make you fishers of men"

(Mark 1:17 NIV). God himself spoke, and they immediately left their nets (their means of livelihood) to go with Him. They obviously saw something in Jesus that was worth sacrificing their security. After Jesus Christ's death and resurrection, they became powerful tools for spreading the Gospel. Through their lives of exercising faith, they gathered together men and women who would, in turn, become followers of Jesus and "fishers of men."

Following God always begins with attitude and perspective, changing hearts from the inside out.

The heart is often the least likely place we tend to consider for some sort of miraculous change to take place. The heart is a metaphor for the most sensitive areas of our lives, the place from which our passions are aroused, but it's also the same place where our worst plans are conceived. God knows how we're wired. The Bible says, "It's in Christ that we find out who we are and what we are living for. Long before we first heard of Christ and got our hopes up, he had his eye on us, had designs on us for glorious living, part of the overall purpose he is working out in everything and everyone" (Ephesians 1:11–12 MSG).

God is a God of love, kindness, and compassion. Scripture says, "I have loved you with an everlasting love; I have drawn you with unfailing kindness" (Jeremiah 31:3 NIV). God is also righteous and just. "The Lord is righteous in all His ways and faithful in all He does" (Psalm 145:17 NIV). Righteousness is a separation from all that is evil unto all that is good. "Yet the Lord longs to be gracious to you; therefore he will rise up to show you compassion. For the Lord is a God of justice. Blessed are all who wait for him!" (Isaiah 30:18 NIV).

Jesus Christ taught the people the truths of God by telling stories. The stories Jesus told are called parables, worldly stories that have a heavenly meaning. Jesus told parables to teach about God, heaven and life in general. You've heard of the Good Samaritan and the lost (prodigal) son, but have you heard of the lost sheep and the Good Shepherd? Parables prompted people to dwell on Jesus' teaching and consider what He said. They are not always easily understood the first time they are heard, but Jesus challenged those who had ears to hear. He said that those that had the desire to understand would be given understanding into the deep things of God. Parables contain much more than just a moral message; parables teach about the character of God and the kingdom of heaven. They comfort us like a bedtime story or keep us guessing like a box-office drama—all the while harboring a spiritual meaning that has the power to change lives.

Following God as the leader is about changing from your worldly perspective to a godly perspective and being transformed from self-focus to God-focus. This kind of radical shift in life's priorities can happen through the power of the Holy Spirit working in our lives. The Bible says, "Those who live according to the sinful nature have their minds set on what that nature desires; but those who live in accordance with the Spirit have their minds set on what the Spirit desires" (Romans 8:5 NIV).

I think if we fail to keep things in a godly perspective, we'll be like Lucy in the *Peanuts* comic strip by Charles Schulz. In one strip, while Lucy swings on the playground, Linus reads to her, "It says here that the world revolves around the sun once a year." Lucy stops abruptly and responds, "The world revolves around the sun? Are you sure? I thought it revolved around me."

Godly Men Choosing to Exercise Faith

God never promised His people a trouble-free life. *David* was a brave shepherd, musician, warrior, king, and a man after God's own heart. The Lord was faithful to David. David went from being the runt of the family to being Israel's greatest king. He always gave God credit for his victories. His journey wasn't an easy one. David sins before God, and God holds him accountable for his actions. David honestly describes his difficulty in a number of psalms in the Bible. "Against you, you only, have I sinned and done what is evil in your sight" (Psalm 51:4 NIV). The psalms are full of declarations about the faithfulness of God. My personal favorite is Psalm 23 in the New King James Version.

A Psalm of David

The Lord is my shepherd;
I shall not want.
He makes me to lie down in green pastures;
He leads me beside the still waters.

He restores my soul;

He leads me in the paths of righteousness

For His name's sake.

Yea, though I walk through the valley of the shadow of death,

I will fear no evil;

For You are with me;

Your rod and Your staff, they comfort me.

You prepare a table before me in the presence of my enemies;

You anoint my head with oil;

My cup runs over.

Surely goodness and mercy shall follow me

All the days of my life;

And I will dwell in the house of the Lord

Forever.

It is a wonderful poem about exercising faith in the living promises of the Shepherd. David closely identifies himself in this world as a sheep who is dependent on the promises of the Good Shepherd—and so should we. Consider David in Psalm 23:1–6. David wonderfully describes the living promises we receive access to when we personally trust and follow God as *my* Shepherd. Not only as *a* Shepherd or *the* Shepherd but as My Shepherd. God promises us every spiritual blessing—something of much more value to our lives than any kind of earthly possessions: verse 1, relationship and supply; verse 2, rest and refreshment; verse 3, healing, guidance, and righteousness; verse 4, protection and comfort; verse 5, provision and anointing;

verse 6, blessing and eternity. Those are His promises to you. Promises He will keep. Developing confidence in the Shepherd sets us free from the past then makes us secure in the present and hopeful for the future. Maybe you've found yourself to be in a challenging position. God promises He will provide for our spiritual needs, as well as our physical ones. He promised to care for us and keep us secure from harm. He gives us peace in the midst of suffering. Because God is faithful, He has never broken a promise.

Job was brutally honest with God about his heartache and questions, and it's important we risk the same vulnerability. The book begins by describing Job as "blameless and upright, he feared God and shunned evil" (Job 1:1). In no time at all, he loses it all, including his ten children. He developed painful sores all over his body. Yet through all this suffering, Job maintained his perspective and did not renounce God. Yet even in his complaints, Job trusts in His redeemer and never abandons his commitment to God or sways from his core values. In the end, the Lord himself came and talked to Job. He restored to Job everything he had formerly possessed and more, but God never explained why he had allowed Job to suffer so terribly. The greatest principle of faith we learn from Job: God is God, and we are not.

One day Saul of Tarsus (later called *Paul*), an enemy of Jesus Christ and his followers, was on a journey to Damascus when God intervened. He heard the voice of Jesus Christ ask why he was persecuting Him. This encounter led to Paul's conversion to Christianity. The apostle Paul proves his Christian faith as he preaches Good News throughout the Mediterranean world and suffers for his faith in Christ. Paul was beaten by rods, stoned unconscious with rocks, chained, imprisoned, and shipwrecked. His writings, which include much of the New Testament, provide a doctrinal foundation of Christianity. Whatever the future holds, Paul tells us that "there is now no condemnation for those who are in Christ Jesus" (Romans 8:1 NIV) and that nothing is "able to separate us from the love of God that is in Christ Jesus our Lord" (Romans 8:39 NIV). Paul's story is a great example of how God and only God can change someone's heart.

The Word of the Lord came to *Jonah*. When God told Jonah to warn the city of Nineveh that he would destroy them if they didn't repent of their evil ways, Jonah wasn't happy. He decided to take the path of his own choosing and boarded a ship that was headed in the opposite direction. Jonah thought he could run away and hide from God. Jonah preferred that God destroy them because he didn't want them to get a second chance. Jonah was guilty of prejudice. A storm and three days in the belly of a large fish helped realign Jonah's perspective. Jonah prayed and was given a second chance, and he obeyed the word of the Lord the second time and went to Nineveh. The Ninevites believed God. More than 120,000 people in the city collectively repented and escaped destruction. Jonah was angry that God was merciful with the Ninevites. The people turned from their evil ways and their violence and were given a second chance. This was the largest three-day revival ever recorded. Jonah makes it clear that, although the Israelites are God's chosen people, they were chosen to be a blessing to other nations. Jesus uses Jonah as an example of the incomprehensible depth of God's love for us. Here's another point to ponder: God is also the God of the first chance.

Habakkuk struggled with God about why God does not put an end to evil. For the prophet lived in a time very similar to our day—a time when everything was in crisis. He lived when there was great national corruption and distress, when the nation and land was filled with hostility, with idolatry, with hatred, and with epidemics of evil. The people are living in wickedness; there is unrest, tragic violence, injustice and oppression throughout the land. Doesn't that sound like today? Habakkuk demanded to know why God didn't seem interested in doing something about the violence and the injustice and the oppression of his nation. God responds, and Habakkuk found a new perspective on life. He acknowledges God is in absolute control. Once Habakkuk made this kind of commitment, he recommitted himself to God. In the midst of difficulty, Habakkuk chose to rejoice and acknowledge God was in control. Habakkuk is a man of God and he knows, and eventually learned the answer to that the fundamental thing to do with a problem—is take it to the one and only true living God. The God who is our strength.

These men came through the pain and the unanswered questions by choosing to exercise faith and focus on the unchanging righteous character of God. We, too, can celebrate

God's power and express delight in God's faithfulness. In this book titled *Hope in a Broken World*, we learn more about the man Habakkuk and how he exercised faith in the midst of affliction. He teaches us five principles of faith, what it looks like and what we need to know, and how we can integrate faith in any kind of injustice and difficulty in our lives. We, too, can rejoice in God, knowing He's in control and that God is the great comforter in all our pain and troubles.

Habakkuk's Story Summary

God commissioned Habakkuk to lead in troubled times. His name means "to embrace," and he earned the title by wrestling with God in the beginning of his book and by developing deep intimacy with God by the book's end. Habakkuk's ministry was during the reign of King Josiah. In the first verse of the book, Habakkuk begins "the burden which the prophet Habakkuk saw." This prophet had seen so much violence and injustice that he felt compelled to cry out to the Lord. "How long, O Lord?" Habakkuk prayed. "How long will I cry to You for help and You do not hear me?" What sets Habakkuk apart from other prophets is he questioned God. Habakkuk's attitude was fearful and questioned God about all the violence that was happening in Judah but nothing having seemed to change. God was listening. He heard Habakkuk's prayers, and He knew what was happening. God answered, "Look around you. Watch! I am doing something amazing, something you wouldn't believe if I told you." Then God told Habakkuk what was going to happen. Habakkuk was confused and perplexed. "Why do it this way, Lord?" Habakkuk asked. God answered, "Write down what I show you. I'm going to show you what will happen in the future. I promise it will happen. Be patient and wait for it. If you are righteous, you will live by faith."

God Is Superior to All Things

The Bible tells us to follow God's ways, not the world's or the way that comes naturally to us. God's ways are different from our ways, and we need to learn from Him. "God's Way is not a matter of mere talk; it's an empowered life" (1 Corinthians 4:20 MSG). God's Word shows us who God is. Throughout the Bible, we see wonderful expressions of God's unconditional love for His people. Paul's work for the church teaches us about the supremacy of God. "This message was kept secret for centuries and generations past, but now it has been revealed to God's people" (Colossians 1:26 New Living Translation).

Christ is the visible image of the invisible God. He existed before anything was created and is supreme over all creation, for through him God created everything in the heavenly realms and on earth. He made the things we can see and the things we can't see—such as thrones, kingdoms, rulers, and authorities in the unseen world. Everything was created through him and for him. He existed before anything else, and he holds all creation together. Christ is also the head of the church, which is his body. He is the beginning, supreme over all who rise from the dead. So he is first in everything. For God in all his fullness was pleased to live in Christ, and through him God reconciled everything to himself. He made peace with everything in heaven and on earth by means of Christ's blood on the cross. This includes you who were once far away from God. You were his enemies, separated from him by your evil thoughts and actions. Yet now he has reconciled you to himself through the death of Christ in his physical body. As a result, he has brought you into his own presence, and you are holy and blameless as you stand before him without a single fault. But you must continue to believe this truth and stand firmly in it. Don't drift away from the assurance you received when you heard the Good News. The Good News has been preached all over the world, and I, Paul, have been appointed as God's servant to proclaim it. (Colossians 1:15–23 NLT)

We must first get an accurate perspective of God. The Holy Bible is the infallible word of God, meaning it is completely trustworthy and true and useful as a guide to exercise faith and accomplish His purpose. What we predominately tend to wrestle with is who God is. The Bible says, "The Word became flesh and made His dwelling among us. We have seen His glory, the glory of the One and Only, who came from the Father, full of grace and truth" (John 1:14 NIV). The Word of God never fails and will stand forever. Jesus is the Word. Jesus is God. He is the Messiah. His name is above every other name.

The second of the Ten Commandments says, "You must not make for yourself an idol of any kind or an image of anything in the heavens or on the earth or in the sea. You must not bow down to them or worship them, for I, the Lord your God, am a jealous God who will not tolerate your affection for any other gods. I lay the sins of the parents upon their children; the entire family is affected—even children in the third and fourth generations of those who reject Me. But I lavish unfailing love for a thousand generations on those who love Me and obey My commands" (Exodus 20:4 NLT).

All the nations surrounding Israel worshipped false gods, whether by a handmade image or through other means. When the Israelites conquered the land, the Lord commanded them to destroy all the places of worship and the images and idols of false religion.

Habakkuk prayed but struggled with why God allowed the people of Judah to get by with their immoral and sinful ways. The Lord replied to his complaint, "But they are deeply guilty, for their own strength is their god" (Habakkuk 1:11 NLT). Since the people of Judah placed their trust in a false god, the city of Jerusalem was eventually burned and destroyed. Numerous people died, and many were taken into captivity by the Babylonians. Christians were warned by Paul and other early church leaders to be on their guard against idolatry.

God has spoken to us in terms we can understand. The Bible is the record of His story and what He wants us to know about Himself. God is spirit, and He does not change. God answers to no one. He does what He pleases and is always right. God's holiness makes it impossible for Him to abuse his absolute power. God cannot go against His own nature. In fact, that is why His promises never fail. All creation is subject to the King of kings and the Lord of lords, and someday everyone and everything will fall down on its knees and worship God—some willingly, some unwillingly. God is the one who brings people and governments to power; He also effects their demise. He is sovereign, meaning He has absolute say over all that goes on earth and His kingdom of heaven. Our God also has absolute rule. He is infinite, eternal, unchanging, and perfect in His nature, attributes, and work. The Bible says that, as a consequence of Adam and Eve's sin, we are all born with a sinful nature that rebels against God and His ways. The Bible says, "You lived in this world without God and without hope" (Ephesians 2:12 NLT). Meaning, it's a world without light, without understanding, without joy. Scripture makes it clear from Genesis to Revelation that God's rule is over all and it is complete and sovereign.

Relationship

The purpose of all things flows from who God is. And essential to who God is, to all His purposes, and to all creation, is His triune nature. God is love and has always been in a relationship. Before the first thing was created, the One God existed in three distinct persons—the Father, the Son, and the Holy Spirit. It's an eternal love relationship that runs so deep and intimate, and the three agree as one. They are a triunity, or trinity.

Relationship is God's highest priority and greatest desire. It should be ours, as well. God deeply desires a love relationship with each of us. That is why He created us. Love is so much more than an emotion. What I mean by that is, God personally demonstrated His love for us by pursuing us in spite of our rejection of Him and our sin. Sin broke the relationship between God and humans. God Himself came to earth to reconcile the broken relationship and give us life. Because God is holy, He also wants us to be holy—to be set apart from the world, chosen to serve Him, and to be blessed by Him. The Bible says, "But just as he called you is holy, so be holy in all you do; for it is written: 'Be holy, because I am holy'" (1 Peter 1:15–16 NIV).

God is both just and merciful, and He desires every person to be saved. "But God demonstrates His own love toward us, in that while we were yet sinners, Christ died for us" (Romans 5:8 New American Standard Bible). God invites us into His story by grace through faith. We develop this relationship with Him in the same way we grow closer to our parents, our spouse, our friends, or to other people—by being together. It's in our response to Him that we exercise faith. The Bible says, "Those who remain in Me, and I in them, will produce much fruit. For apart from Me you can do nothing. Anyone who does not remain in Me is thrown away like a useless branch and withers" (John 15:5 NLT).

Vital Need for Survival

The Bible says there is only one way to God. Jesus said, "I am the way and the truth and the life. No one comes to the Father except through me" (John 14:6 NIV). Our identity is found in Christ alone. Our future and our hope are in Him, not in the ways of this world, the economy, our financial status, or our political affiliations. The Bible tells us, "In Him we have redemption in His blood, the forgiveness of our trespasses, according to the riches of His grace which He lavished on us. In all wisdom and insight" (Ephesians 1:7 NASB). Enthusiasm for Jesus Christ and exercising faith are both potent "lures" for the gospel. Jesus offered living water to all those who were spiritually thirsty.

Remember the Samaritan woman at the well? Within a few hours after meeting Jesus Christ, the woman at the well was exercising her newfound faith by telling everyone she knew what He had done in her life. She had no evangelical training, but her enthusiastic expression of the evidence led many of her fellow Samaritans to believe in Jesus. Jesus said, "Whoever drinks the water I give him will never thirst. Indeed, the water I give him will become in him a spring welling up to eternal life" (John 4:14 NIV). God is the only one who can satisfy our spiritual thirst. After we drink from what He offers, we'll never again be spiritually dead. When you follow God as leader, like sheep following a shepherd, you are exercising faith that He will guide you safely to your destination.

Leadership and Faith

Many of the Bible's greatest leaders were trained for leadership by serving under leaders themselves. Some served under godly leaders, such as Paul under Barnabas and Joshua under Moses. Others served under difficult leaders, like David under Saul and Daniel under Nebuchadnezzar. David worked under Saul, the current king with diligence and respect, even when Saul became jealous and wanted to kill him. David twice had the opportunity to kill Saul and take the throne that had been promised to him, but he refused to do anything against "the Lord's anointed" (1 Samuel 24:6 NIV). From both the positive and negative examples, we learn to exercise leadership in a godly way.

There exists no better example of a godly leader than the Lord Jesus Christ. Jesus is our spiritual leader. He was not a religious leader. He was not a political leader either. Jesus is Lord, meaning He is owner. He ultimately is leader of all. He is God's son, the holder of ultimate power, who humbled himself by becoming an obedient human being and by dying for sins He didn't commit. Jesus said, "I am the good shepherd. The good shepherd lays down his life for the sheep" (John 10:11 NIV). In the sixth verse of Psalms 23, David says, the Shepherd leads His sheep every step of the way until they are home. We are called to be close to Him and under His command.

In the Gospel of Matthew, the Roman soldier understood more clearly than many of us today the principle of leadership and faith. He knew how to exercise it and how to be under it. In other words, he knew how to follow God as the leader. That's why he responded so directly to the leadership he saw in Jesus. Those of us who want to have leadership first need to know how to be under authority. Following God as leader is lived out by serving under His authority.

If you are in leadership, model yourself after Jesus. Be approachable. Don't fight back if you're verbally attacked, and look for ways to help others in need. Follow the greatest commandment: "Love the Lord your God with all your heart and with all your soul and with all your mind" (Matthew 22:37 NIV).

It's easy to exercise faith when things are going well, but how about when tough times come? Jesus said, "In this world you will have trouble. But take heart! I have overcome the world" (John 16:33 NIV). Faith is essential to eternal life. Only the God of the Bible, the one who sent His son, Jesus Christ, to die on the cross for our sins, is fully trustworthy. "There is salvation in no one else! God has given no other name under heaven by which we must be saved" (Acts 4:12 NLT). We can't save ourselves from the effects and consequences of sin. Thankfully, God executed the rescue operation for salvation. He sent His son to save the world by paying the penalty for sin and bringing us back to God. Jesus's name means "God rescues." Because we cannot see God now, we live our lives by faith.

John the Baptist leaped in his mother's womb at the sound of Mary's pregnant voice and received the Holy Spirit. John the Baptist was Jesus's cousin, the son of Zachariah and Elizabeth. John played a critical role in the life of Jesus Christ on earth. His name came from the ministry of baptizing people who were returning to the ways of God. His life was prophesied about hundreds of years before his birth.

John was set apart from birth, meaning he was "in" the world but was not "of" the world. He was not conformed to this world. The name John means "the Lord is gracious." He certainly is. John lived outside the city walls of Jerusalem and baptized people on the other side of the Jordan. He lived out in the wilderness. He was known as an outsider, an outcast, a cultural misfit. The truth is, the wilderness is a spiritual place where all God's ambassadors live out their faith in Him until we (His people) return home and receive our full inheritance in heaven.

John the Baptist was given the most amazing task to carry out. He was to reveal to the people of Israel whom the Messiah is. Can you imagine the thrill it must've been to be the first one to witness that? What an amazing responsibility. Only one problem: John had no idea who the Messiah was.

John walked by faith, not by sight. John had a specific message: to preach repentance and to baptize people with water for the forgiveness of sins in preparation for the coming of the Son of God so that through Him, all men might believe. John said, "After me will come one more powerful than I, the thongs of whose sandals I am not worthy to stoop down and untie. I baptize you with water, but He will baptize you with the Holy Spirit" (Mark 1:7–8 NIV).

All the people of Jerusalem went out to the desert region, the Jordan River where John was baptizing. At that time, John saw Jesus coming toward him and said, "Look, the Lamb of God, who takes away the sin of the world" (John 1:29 NIV)! Jesus is baptized in the Jordan River. Then John gave this testimony:

> I saw the Spirit come down from heaven as a dove and remain on Him. I would not have known him, except that the one who sent me to baptize with water told me. 'The man on whom you see the Spirit come down and remain is He who will baptize with the Holy Spirit.' I have seen and I testify that this is the Son of God. (John 1:32–34 NIV)

Faith is trusting the certainty of what God says. The next day, Jesus was passing by and John the Baptist said to his two disciples, Andrew and John, "Look, the Lamb of God!" John made known the Messiah and immediately the two men followed Jesus.

God is always working for our good in every situation, even in those situations that seem to be working against us. John the Baptist was arrested and bound because of his preaching. While in prison and bewildered, John questioned whether Jesus was the Messiah. John sent a couple men to the Lord to ask if He was the one to come or should we expect someone else.

The Lord replied, "Go back and report to John what you have seen and heard: The blind receive sight, the lame walk, those who have leprosy are cured, the deaf hear, the dead are raised, and the good news is preached to the poor" (Luke 7:22 NIV). Jesus reassured John that He was indeed the Savior of the world. The Shepherd's words bring great comfort when we are hurting, confused, or when we have run-ins with difficulty and pain. Because we belong to God, we can rejoice even during tough times—not because situations work out the way we want but because our future is in the hands of the One who loves the Son and takes great joy in those that lift Him up above their selfish desires. "Whoever believes in the Son has eternal life, but whoever rejects the Son will not see life, for God's wrath remains on them" (John 3:36 NIV).

King Herod called for the beheading of John the Baptist. One of the great examples of faith we learn from John the

Baptist is how he showed true humility by setting aside his pride to honor and follow God as the leader. John the Baptist is a witness to Jesus Christ's coming and His power. Therefore, this joy of mine is fulfilled. "He must increase, but I must decrease" (John 3:30 NKJV).

We read over and over in the Bible that God pulls down those who exalt themselves and lifts up those who are humble. As we put our faith in the truth of who Jesus is and what He has done for us, we have access to the power to say "no" to anything that would grieve Him and "yes" to all that pleases Him.

Prayer and Love for the Brokenhearted

Habakkuk teaches us to pray to the living God and that it's okay to ask God questions. Habakkuk didn't debate his viewpoint or argue with God by defending his position. He asked detailed and specific questions. He asked how God could allow the people to continue sinning and disobeying Him. Prayer, simply put, is talking to God. Habakkuk submitted himself under the authority of Almighty God. We should enjoy such intimacy with God that we can openly express our questions, concerns, or confusion over God's ways.

Prayer is also confessing our sins and thanking Him for what He's done. Be humble but persistent when you pray. The Bible says, "But when you pray, go into your room, close the door and pray to your Father, who is unseen. Then your Father, who sees what is done in secret, will reward you" (Matthew 6:6

NIV). When Jesus Christ was on the earth, he always took time out to talk to the Father. If the son of God himself needed to pray, how much more do we. He made over seventy statements in His Word about prayer. When you spend time in prayer, you are exercising faith that God is listening to your hopes and dreams, as well as your burdens and requests. In those times when it seems like God isn't listening, we are to keep praying. God is intimate with us when we pray, and He is always listening.

Maybe, if you're like me, you've experienced times in your life when they're lonely to live in, we go through hard times, and feeling like God is distant. Because of sin, troubling times are inevitable. Such events can cause distress or worry or anxiety. They can also provide opportunities to pray and develop your relationship with the Lord. God is the answer to our pain and troubles. Praying with faith implies staying connected with God, ready to take any opportunity He brings for us to serve and obey Him. When we lack confidence, we need God's Word to remind us of His faithfulness. Remembering what King David wrote, "Even though I walk through the valley of the shadow of death, I fear no evil, for You are with me; Your rod and Your staff, they comfort me" (Psalm 23:4 NASB).

God, the creator of the heavens and the earth, is on your side. If anyone tries to convince you otherwise, don't be deceived. We all experience adversity in our lives. But in any uncertain, stressful, or pandemic situation like the one we all experienced with COVID-19, we've got the upper hand. "I will fear no evil, for You are with me" (Psalm 23:4 NKJV). Who can be against us when we have that kind of backup? God promised to protect and comfort us in these uncertain times. God always keeps His promises. The alternative is being disconnected from God, consumed with our own interests, and fearful of the unknown.

Ever wonder why the Shepherd carries a rod and a hook-like staff? Sheep stumble down ledges, fall into crevices, get stuck in hedges, and thorny brushes. It's not uncommon for sheep to plunge into deep ravines and pits. Sheep need the Shepherd's rod to keep them on the right path and fight off predators when they try to attack. God is always there to pull us out of complex situations. His watchful eye brings comfort.

When we pray, He hears both our words and the emotions and needs behind them. The Bible says, "And the Holy Spirit helps us in our weakness. For example, we don't know what God wants us to pray for. But the Holy Spirit prays for us with groanings that cannot be expressed with words" (Romans 8:26 NLT). When we lack answers, we ought to follow God as the leader, seeking His wisdom. When we seek godly wisdom, we are exercising faith, meaning biblical wisdom through action. The Bible tells us, "Do not merely listen to the word, and so deceive yourselves, Do what it says" (James 1:22 NIV). When you give your heart to God, He gives you the Holy Spirit, who comes to live in your heart. As followers of Christ, we are baptized to be transformed by the Holy Spirit. Transformation occurs when we daily submit to the Holy Spirit. That's exercising faith!

God restores the brokenhearted. For the most part, broken means useless until repaired. Jesus went up on a mountainside and began to teach, "Blessed are the poor in spirit, for theirs is the kingdom of heaven" (Matthew 5:3 NASB). What this means is, because of sin, we are "spiritually poor" in our relationship with God. There is absolutely nothing we can do to reconcile this relationship. Jesus said, "With man this is impossible, but not with God; all things are possible with God" (Mark 10:27 NIV). Yet because God can work all things together for good, even broken things have value. For instance, proud people sometimes need to be broken or humbled before they realize they need to change. I was one of them. David explains, "The sacrifice You desire is a broken spirit. You will not reject a broken and repentant heart, O God" (Psalm 51:17 NLT).

The NIV Starting Point Study Bible says, it's encouraging to know that God takes broken hearts and spirits and gently mends, heals, and shapes them. Worries or burdens weigh heavily on our hearts, often making it difficult to enjoy each day. God knows this, so in His great love, He lifts and bears our burdens. He tells us to take our burdens to Him so He can carry them. God calls us to help lighten each other's burdens, as well. We are to encourage and instruct each other from Scripture and, above all else, love each other. Jesus explained, "Love the Lord your God with all your heart and with all your soul and with all your mind. This is the first and greatest commandment. And the second is like it: Love your neighbor as yourself. All the law and the Prophets hang on these two commandments" (Matthew 22:37–40 NIV).

Takeaway: Studying His word, walking with Him in faith, and seeking Him gets me back to where I should be, in right relationship, serving under His authority and glorifying Him.

Memory Verse: "There is salvation in no one else! God has given no other name under heaven by which we must be saved" (Acts 4:12 NLT).

Question to Think About: In spite of all the injustice, suffering, and difficulty around you in this broken world, how can I exercise faith by following under the authority of God as my Lord and leader?

_____

_____

_____

_____

_____

_____

_____

_____

PRINCIPLE 1

PRINCIPLE 2

Always Wait for His Instruction

In the morning, Lord, you hear my voice; in the morning
I lay my requests before you and wait expectantly.
—Psalm 5:3 NIV

In the Old Testament, God provided manna each morning for the people of Israel. But shortly before this took place, the whole congregation of the people grumbled against Moses and Aaron in the wilderness. They were complaining and quarreling because of their failure to rest in Him and wait for His instruction. Patience is an expression of godliness and love.

God told Moses to tell the people, "Look, I'm going to rain down food from heaven for you. Each day the people can go out and pick up as much food as they need for that day. I will test them in this to see whether or not they will follow My instructions" (Exodus 16:4 NLT). When Jesus said, "I am the bread of life" (John 6:48 NIV), He was comparing Himself to the manna God sent the Israelites when they had no food. Just as bread is the physical food that keeps us alive, Jesus is the spiritual food that can give us eternal life if we believe He was sent to die for our sins. Jesus Christ used bread as a symbol of His body being broken in death. Jesus commanded His disciples to do this the night before He was crucified. Christians remember Christ's death by "breaking bread" and eating bread together during Communion service, or the Lord's Supper.

Problems and Dependence

Since the fall of man, humanity has attempted to achieve heaven through religion, good works, morality, ability, prosperity, philosophy, and self-righteousness. Unfortunately, humanity is spending forever trying to understand who we are rather than understanding who God is. That's the problem! Humanity is bent on going anywhere except in the direction it should be heading. My pastor and mentor, the late Tom Shrader, founding pastor of Redemption Church, Gilbert, Arizona, was asked, "What is the purpose of the church?" Tom responded, "The purpose of the church is not to solve people's problems. God didn't give you problems to get them fixed. He didn't give you problems to get them solved. God gave you problems to drive you to Him." Take time out right now to praise God for His faithfulness, and ask God to help you confess the real motives of your heart. The truth is, God's kindness often involves difficulty and even suffering to bring us to our knees. You may right now be saying to yourself, "I don't have a problem." The mere thought of you acknowledging you don't have a problem is a problem! The real issue of why we have problems is *sin*. Life in a broken world is full of problems. Every day, we are confronted with a different reality—the evil and suffering brought on by a world living without God. The Bible says:

> We can rejoice, too, when we run into problems and trials, for we know that they help us develop endurance. And endurance develops strength of character, and character strengthens our confident hope of salvation. And this hope will not lead to disappointment. For we know how dearly God loves us, because He has given us the Holy Spirit to fill our hearts with His love. (Romans 5:3–5 NLT)

The problem of sin is no light matter. The law of Moses reveals our sin and how short we fall from meeting God's standard. The Bible says, "the wages of sin is death" (Romans 6:23 NASB). We need a Savior. God sent His own Son, Jesus Christ, to earth as the Lamb of God and became the sacrificial lamb to our problems. Sin can only be solved by death, the shedding of innocent blood. Jesus had to die a sinner's death to deal with our problem of sin. Jesus emptied Himself and paid the ultimate price—for the church. There was absolutely nothing we could do to get to heaven, so God came to live with people on earth and obey the law perfectly and die for the sins of His people. The innocent blood of Jesus covers our guilt, allowing us into God's kingdom for eternity. We can trust in Him for salvation. Jesus said, "Come to Me, all you who are weary and carry heavy burdens, and I will give you rest" (Matthew 11:28 NLT). God Himself became the sacrificial lamb to our problems. This ultimately explains the cross of Jesus Christ. It is finished.

The Bible says separation from God is like being lost. That means people wander through life without accepting God's plan. We do not know what man is meant to be. We are blind to our own understanding and lost our sense of direction here upon the earth. God's Word is the instructional manual that provides the truth of who we really are and who we actually can be. "What is truth? God is truth. Everything He says we can believe. There is no deception, no hypocrisy, no half-truth in God. Whatever He does and commands us to do is right. Anything God hates and forbids us to do is wrong. We will never be able to fully comprehend God or understand all His mysteries, but he is everything He says He is: the all-powerful, just, loving Creator of everything that exists" (Luis Palau).

Many young adults, on the other hand, get encouraged by their parents to go and try to find their own independence in this world. But here's how that usually goes: Young adults leave home on a quest to conquer the world (with seemingly good intentions, by the way). They begin on a path of their own choosing, to explore their own level of freedom, squandering their money on foolish worldly desires and pleasures, but when (not if) but when they come to a crossroads or, worse, a dead-end, they try to make sense of why they feel completely alone in life, with no sense of direction or purpose. The answer is found in Genesis 3, the Fall of Man. Adam and Eve ignored God's voice and decided to go their own way. When they acted on that decision to sin, they immediately alienated themselves from God, from one another, and from the rest of creation. But God had a master plan. Paul explains, "For the sin of this one man, Adam, brought death to many. But even greater is God's wonderful grace and His gift of forgiveness to many through this other man, Jesus Christ" (Romans 5:17 NLT).

In his written commentary of Chapter 3 of Genesis, "The Enticement of Evil," Pastor Ray C. Stedman observes:

> We come to Chapter 3 of Genesis with a heightened sense of anticipation. In many ways this is the most important piece of information ever conveyed to man. Here is the ultimate explanation for the tensions this morning among the nations over the Korean incident, or the war in Vietnam. Here we have the answer to the eternal "Why" that arises in our hearts in

times of tragedy or sorrow. Here is the explanation for over a hundred centuries of human heartache, misery, torture, blood, sweat, and tears. Here is the reason for the powerful fascination that LSD and marijuana hold for young people today; for the passion for power and the lure of wealth and the enticements of forbidden sex, to young and old alike. Here is the only reasonable answer for the existence of these things in the world today.

This independence scheme offers a false sense of security, happiness, and fulfillment. Many young adults search for fulfillment through substitutes such as food, drugs, alcohol, sex, money, work, or social media outlets. But ultimately, only Jesus can satisfy. Jesus said, "I am the bread of life" (John 6:48 NASB). Like bread nourishes our bodies, Jesus's unconditional love satisfies our souls. Substitutes are like candy; they taste sweet, but they never really satisfy our hunger. Jesus said, "I am the living bread that came down from heaven. If anyone eats of this bread, he will live forever. This bread is my flesh, which I will give for the life of the world" (John 6:51 NIV). The spiritual intimacy Jesus desires with each of us satisfies every longing of our hearts now and throughout eternity. For that reason, God is drawing us to Himself as we learn to rely on Him and give our fears and worries to Him, realizing our total dependence on our heavenly Father.

Trials

The Bible says, the paths we choose to take have immediate and long-term consequences. If we are not paying attention, we may wake up one day and discover we have arrived somewhere we never intended to go. Our perspective on trials can be positive or negative, and it ultimately affects the outcome of our hardship. Hard times help us learn; they stretch and challenge us. When we are confronted by a trial and realize our limitations, God is glorified. God never leaves us during our hard times; He gives us the perseverance and faith necessary to match our trials. "In fact, everyone who wants to live a godly life in Christ Jesus will be persecuted, while evil men and imposters will go from bad to worse, deceiving and being deceived" (2 Timothy 3:12–13). Sometimes, following the Lord's commands brings harsh consequences, endangering not only our comfort but also our safety. Through these times, we know that God will be with us. God's plan always have our good in mind. "For I know the plans I have for you," declares the Lord, "plans to prosper you and not to harm you, plans to give you hope and a future" (Jeremiah 29:11 NIV).

The Bible's most vivid illustration of this is the account of Job. In a single day, his wealth was obliterated, and his children were killed. Later, he lost his health. Those closest to him challenged his faith: his wife ordered him to curse God, and his friends insisted a hidden sin had brought about his woes. Yet Job persevered, remaining loyal to his faith and the knowledge of his relationship with God. God later rewarded him for such faithfulness.

"God does not give you more than you can handle." Though this saying never appears in the Bible, there is a lot of biblical truth to it. Our character becomes more like Christ's through difficulty and suffering. God does not leave us alone in our suffering. God will give us faith and strength to match the trials and difficulties that inevitably trickles into our lives. The Bible says, "Consider it pure joy, my brothers, whenever you face trials of many kinds, because you know that the testing of your faith develops perseverance" (James 1:2–3 NIV). The Bible tells us that, since Jesus was tempted, He can also help us resist temptation. It also says that God will never allow us to be tempted beyond what we can bear. When we resist temptation, our faith in God grows stronger.

Obedience, Time, and Grace

God's ways are different from our ways, and we need to learn and obey His instruction. God declares, "For as the heavens are higher than the earth, so are My ways higher than your ways And My thoughts than your thoughts" (Isaiah 55:9 NASB). Obedience means doing what God says no matter how unpopular, puzzling, or difficult the command is. Although doing what God says can be difficult at times, God has every right as our Creator to demand our obedience. He gives each of us remarkable personal freedom and responsibility, and yet

He is still able to guide the overall direction of human events. When we obey Him willingly from a heart that trusts Him, our obedience is a gift of love to Him. "For this is the love of God, that we keep His commandments, and His commandments are not burdensome. For whatever is born of God overcomes the world; and this is the victory that has overcome the world—our faith" (1 John 5:3–4 NASB). The Lord says that this kind of gift means more to Him than any other sacrifice we can make.

> Whoever is not with Me is against me, and whoever does not gather with Me, scatters. When an impure spirit comes out of a person, it goes through arid places seeking rest and does not find it. Then it says, 'I will return to the house I left.' When it arrives, it finds the house swept clean and put in order. Then it goes and takes seven other spirits more wicked than itself, and they go in and live there. And the final condition of that person is worse than the first." As Jesus was saying these things, a woman in the crowd called out, "Blessed is the mother who gave you birth and nursed you." He replied, "Blessed rather are those who hear the word of God and obey it. (Luke 11:23–28 NASB)

God never wastes our experiences, especially the painful ones. No matter what the situation, he turns trials around and uses them for good in our lives and in the lives of others. The Bible says, "Blessed is the one who perseveres under trial because, having stood the test, that person will receive the crown of life that the Lord has promised to those who love Him" (James 1:12 NIV). Sometimes, God may require us to put our dreams on hold until the proper time. His timing is perfect and always results in good things. Other times when we ask God to free us from our circumstances, we have to wait until He has completed His purpose for us there. God often uses such times to heal other areas of our lives that we didn't know were broken. As His followers, God's plans always have our good in mind. He knows that these plans are for our best interest, but He does not force them on us. He loves us so much that He encourages us to embrace them. "And we know that God causes all things to work together for the good of those who love God and are called according to His purpose for them" (Romans 8:28 NLT).

Despite Jonah's disobedience, his stubbornness, his lack of perspective, his cultural prejudice, his self-righteousness, his wrong motives, and his bad attitude, God never gave up on him. The greatest example of faith we learn from Jonah: sometimes, God uses us, in spite of us, to accomplish His gracious mission. I happen to believe there's a little Jonah in us all. Now is the time to follow Jesus Christ. In the Bible, He warned that all people should live for Him because the time is coming when

He will return to the earth. The truth is God invites us into His redemption story by grace through faith in His perfect timing, for His good pleasure. God promises He will provide for our spiritual needs, as well as our physical ones.

> Do this, knowing the time, that it is already the hour for you to awaken from sleep; for now salvation is nearer to us than when we believed. The night is almost gone, and the day is near. Therefore let us lay aside the deeds of darkness and put on the armor of light. Let us behave properly as in the day, not in carousing and drunkenness, not in sexual promiscuity and sensuality, not in strife and jealousy. But put on the Lord Jesus Christ, and make no provision for the flesh in regard to its lusts. (Romans 13:11–14 NASB)

Failure to obey expresses a disbelief in our Lord's ability to meet all our needs, and it suggests that we think we can do a better job than our shepherd is doing for us. God is the great provider. But that doesn't mean we get everything we want. What it does mean is that God will provide everything He thinks we need. God is not opposed to our having houses, cars, clothes, and other possessions, but he doesn't want them to become our obsession. Jesus declared, "What good is it for a man to gain the whole world, yet forfeit his soul?" We may not be aware of all the things we allow to take precedence over obedience to Him. But if we listen to God, He will help us identify the idols of our heart and displace those things. We need to learn to let go and let God. In Psalm 46:10 the Lord directs us to "Cease striving and know that I am God." When we surrender our lives to God and give Him control of the things that control us, like money, power, ambition, and physical desires, His resurrection life flows into us and breaks the bonds of fear, sin, and addictive habits.

The Bible tells us that the only thing people deserve from God is punishment because all of us have sinned. "For all have sinned and fall short of the glory of God" (Romans 3:23 NIV). God will never approve of the wrong things we do, and he will not tolerate continued disobedience. But God the Father has accepted Christ's death as payment for the sins of anyone who trusts in Jesus as Savior. It is only because of God's grace that we do not receive what we deserve. Instead, God offers eternal life as a free gift. "For the wages of sin is death, but the free gift of God is eternal life in Christ Jesus our Lord" (Romans 6:23 NASB). God's grace is evident in His mercy. He often delays punishment in order to give us time to turn to Him. Because of God's grace, He provided Jesus Christ as a sacrifice so our sins could be forgiven.

Takeaway: His timing is perfect and always results in good things.

Memory Verse: "And we know that God causes all things to work together for the good of those who love God and are called according to His purpose for them" (Romans 8:28 NLT).

Question to Think About: In what areas of my life do I need to let go and let God?

_____

_____

_____

_____

_____

_____

_____

_____

_____

PRINCIPLE 2

PRINCIPLE 3

Immediately Listen to His Voice

We love because He first loved us.

—1 John 4:19

The Bible compares people to sheep and God to a shepherd. Our dependence rests on the shepherd's protection and guidance. When we declare we are followers of God, we are exercising faith that we are fully submitted to the Lord and Shepherd, with an understanding that He is owner and perfecter of our faith. Jesus said, "My sheep hear my voice, and I know them, and they follow me, and I give eternal life to them, and they will never perish; and no one will snatch them out of My hand" (John 10:27–28 NASB). This scripture should bring great comfort to your soul. Although sheep are not known for their intelligence and power, we need a shepherd to protect us, keep us secure from harm, and care for us. Jesus Christ called himself the Good Shepherd. He seeks His sheep, and they recognize Him as their Shepherd. If you really want to please and obey Him, you'll stay humble; He promises to guide you. Don't make guidance complicated. Our response to His love is to go directly to Him, either by prayer or by His written word. The Bible says, "Faith comes from hearing, that is, hearing the Good News about Christ" (Romans 10:17 NLT). We are to wait patiently for His instruction and immediately listen to His voice. Without God, we're like lost sheep in need of a shepherd to care for us.

Even though we highly respect others' views, we must be diligent to examine scriptures for ourselves. God's message came to Ezekiel, and he explains who the "true shepherd" is in chapter 34:

> God, the Master, says: From now on, I myself am the shepherd. I'm going looking for them. As shepherds go after their flocks when they get scattered, I'm going after my sheep. I'll rescue them from all the places they've been scattered to in the storms. I'll bring them back to their home country. I'll feed them on the mountains of Israel, along the streams, among their own people. I'll lead them into lush pasture so they can roam the mountain pastures of Israel, graze at leisure, feed in the rich pastures on the mountains of Israel. And I myself will be the shepherd of my sheep. I

myself will make sure they get plenty of rest. I'll go after the lost, I'll collect the strays, I'll doctor the injured, I'll build up the weak ones and oversee the strong ones so they're not exploited. (Ezekiel 34:11–16 the Message)

Sheep are stubborn animals and prone to getting lost, meaning like people, they will go anywhere except in the direction they should be heading. Sheep are defenseless and entirely dependent on the shepherd for guidance and protection. If one sheep decides to run off a cliff, they all go. There are three reasons why sheep wander: (1) they take their eye off the shepherd, (2) they follow other sheep onto wrong paths, (3) they take the path of their own choosing. Think about the last message you heard. Don't take their word for it; take the time to consider it in the light of God's Word. But don't get me wrong. Allow God to speak to you in the way He chooses. Ask Him to help you silence your own thoughts and desires and opinions of others that may be filling your mind. If you find yourself stuck in an unusual situation and you're not sure what to do, turn your focus to the Master. After asking your question, wait for Him to answer. Hearing the voice of the Good Shepherd is a basic right of every child of God.

Condition of the Heart

While Habakkuk waited, God did a wonderful work in his heart. When his prayers seemed to go unanswered, God spoke! And something changed. He wasn't prepared for God's resolution. His first flinch was to question God why. Triumphantly, God even uses violent people to punish other violent people, something the prophet Habakkuk struggled to understand. What was at stake here is the condition of Habakkuk's heart. God answered, with a promise. The one thing that changed? His perspective! God opened the eyes and ears of Habakkuk's heart. Habakkuk realized he must first be a listener. Listening is a learned skill. We, too, may learn to keep our hearts open to change. God is always working in the hearts of His people. When Habakkuk acknowledged God's plan for the future, it trumped what he felt. Habakkuk once felt perplexed; now he has peace. He once felt confused; now he has contentment. He once felt fearful; now he has faith in the future God has planned.

In the New Testament, Jesus Christ explained, "Why do you look at the speck of sawdust in your brother's eye and pay no attention to the plank in your own eye? How can you say to your brother, 'Let me take the speck out of your eye,' when all the time there is a plank in your own eye. You hypocrite first take the plank out of your own eye, and then you will see clearly to remove the speck from your brother's eye" (Matthew 7:3–5 NIV). This scripture speaks directly to the heart of the issue. God's concern is the condition of the heart. Jesus further explained, "Are you still lacking in understanding also? Do you not understand that everything that goes into the mouth passes into the stomach, and is eliminated? But the things that proceed out of the mouth come from the heart, and those defile the man. For out of the man come evil thoughts, murders, adulteries, fornications, thefts, false witness, slanders. These are the things that defile" (Matthew 15:16–20 NASB).

On one occasion, the disciples set sail in a boat to the other side of the lake. Jesus Christ amazed His disciples when He displayed His power over fierce winds and raging seas. His disciples felt fearful of drowning and woke Him up from sound sleep. He spoke, and the winds immediately quieted, and the waters grew calm. "Where is your faith?" Jesus asked. He was testing His disciples, even in troubling conditions, to exercise faith. God is a heart examiner! God can see the hearts of humankind, and He examines them to determine those who really love and obey Him. It is important not only for God to examine our lives but for us to examine our own lives, as well, from hidden sin. When we admit our sin and turn from it, we can expect forgiveness and a restoration of uninterrupted fellowship with God. Sometimes, our feelings of guilt and unworthiness may keep us from God. It's true we don't deserve God's forgiveness, but He, in His irresistible grace, continually showers us with undeserved blessings. He wants us to go to Him, no matter what our condition.

How do you examine the word of truth? There are times we discuss biblical issues as if we were playing the childhood game of telephone. Over the years, my wife and I would play this game with our kids in Sunday-school class. The kids thought it was fun, enlightening, and usually provided a good laugh at the end. In that game, participants sit in a circle, and the leader whispers a sentence to the person on the right. As the sentence is whispered from child to child, words are unintentionally dropped or altered. By the time the sentence has gone full circle, it often bears little resemblance to the original. Sometimes, what we "know" of the Bible is achieved in a similar way. Whereas the childhood game was a source of amusement, the same methodology can be disastrous in biblical studies. We all too easily mimic a friend's comments, a teacher, the pastor's sermon, or maybe it was something passed down from generation to generation. God helps those who help themselves! Such hand-me-down understanding and secondhand wisdom can be subject to glaring gaps and deadly distortions.

God speaks in different ways. He may choose to speak to you through His word. This could come in your daily reading of the Bible, or he could guide you to a particular verse. "For the Word of God is alive and active. Sharper than any two-edged sword, it penetrates even to dividing soul and spirit, joints and marrow, it judges the thoughts and attitudes of the heart" (Hebrews 4:12 NIV). He may also speak to you through dreams, through visions, or through other people. But probably the most common way is through the quiet inner voice. The point of scripture is not intended to intimidate you; it's so we can get an accurate view of God. I once listened to a charismatic preacher on television who spoke something into my spirit. He said, "The Bible doesn't make sense, it makes faith." This quote has remained with me ever since. It has taught me that faith is not a mental exercise; it always proves itself real by how we live our lives.

Every time we pray, we are confident that He is listening and that He will answer. We live out this trust by making decisions based on what God says is true, rather than by what we feel or think. Ask God for wisdom and insight, and seek the counsel of godly people. If you want to evaluate a voice you've heard, use this simple test: Does it exalt Jesus as Lord? Does it affirm the truth of scripture? Does it lead to a growing freedom and maturity in Christ? If it does, keep listening, for God is speaking. We know that God sees the future even more clearly than we see the present. God can see the hearts of humankind, and He examines them to determine those who really love and obey Him. "Test me, O Lord, and try me, examine my heart and my mind" (Psalm 26:2 NIV). God tests us, but we are not to test Him.

Testimony of Faith

Faith means to trust Him with our unknowns, even in our most confusing times. For example, in the fall of 2003, I accepted a job transfer to Grapevine, Texas. My wife, Laura, and our three young children remained in Arizona until the home sold and I became settled in. Soon, my life was spiraling out of control. It continued to revolve around a self-centered, self-seeking heart and a mind trying to figure out this life on my own. I was a functioning alcoholic.

On Sunday evening, broken and confused, I called out to a God I didn't know, ashamed of who I was and who I had become, and asked for a miracle. On Monday afternoon, my life was forever changed the moment I met Christ for the first time. I was dead in my sins and trespasses, and God breathed life into my mortal body. A flash of light turned on in the inside of me, but I was still somewhat confused and didn't know what was happening. I sat down on the corner of the bed and checked my pulse.

On Wednesday, something went wrong to the engine of my SUV and needed to be removed and replaced. On Friday of that week, I walked over to my coworker's desk and vented my long list of troubles. That is when without breaking eye contact, my coworker reached underneath her desk and handed me a Bible already opened to the book of James and said, "Here's where you need to start reading!"

I was taken back. I had never opened a Bible before, let alone have one opened for me. I carried it over to my desk and started reading. His Word wasn't what I expected. The Word opened the eyes of my heart, and scriptures seemed to pop off the page—I couldn't put it down. After I read the book of James, I walked back over to my coworker's desk to thank her and said, "This book is amazing!" I had never before read a book from start to finish in my life. I shared my enthusiasm about how the Spirt of God revealed what I experienced earlier in the week. It was the holy presence of God that entered my body.

After several minutes of rambling on and on, I looked up and observed my coworker bawling her eyes out.

A month later, the organization graciously accepted my transfer back to Arizona. On my drive home, the Lord revealed to me, just like the engine of my car needed replacing, He also needed to remove and replace my old callous heart with a new one.

Before leaving town, my coworker gave me a CD filled with a variety of Christian songs. I listened to it in the SUV and sang my little heart out with tears of joy and thanksgiving all the way home to my family in Arizona. On it was a song performed by Bart Millard of the band Mercy Me. The song is titled, "Crazy." It has become one of my all-time favorites because it reminds me of a time of mounting trials, suffering and confusion, but how God extended His saving grace and miracle mercy to me and led me in a completely different direction. Here's how the lyrics go:

Why would I spend my life longing
for the day that it would end
Why would I spend my time pointing to another man
Isn't that crazy
How can I find hope in dying with promises unseen
How can I learn Your way is better in
everything I'm taught to be
Isn't that crazy

I have not been called to the wisdom of this world
But to a God who's calling out to me
And even though the world may think
I'm losing touch with reality

It would be crazy to choose this world
Over eternity

And if I boast let me boast in filthy rags made clean
And if I glory let me glory in my Savior's suffering
Isn't that crazy
And as I live this daily life I trust You for everything
And I will only take a step when I feel You leading me
Isn't that crazy

I have not been called to the wisdom of this world
But to a God who's calling out to me
And even though the world may think
I'm losing touch with reality
It would be crazy to choose this world
Over eternity

I encourage you to find some alone time with God and meditate on these lyrics as well. As a Spirit-filled Christian, I learned to trust God in difficult and confusing times and lean not on my own understanding. The Bible says, "The wind blows wherever it pleases. You hear its sound, but you cannot tell where it comes from or where it is going. So it is with everyone born of the Spirit" (John 3:8 NIV). Once you are born again, your Spirit is brought to life and lives on for eternity, even when your physical life ends. True victory comes when you focus on God, intentionally listen to His voice in everything you do, quickly respond to it, in spite of our pain or our questions.

Takeaway: God is always working in the hearts of His people.

Memory Verse: "My sheep hear my voice, and I know them, and they follow me, and I give eternal life to them, and they will never perish; and no one will snatch them out of My hand" (John 10:27–28 NASB).

Question to Think About: How often do you make it a priority to spend the first part of your day with God? Take time right now to ask God to help you. What comes to mind? Write it down, then lift it up in prayer to God (out loud).

_____

_____

_____

_____

_____

_____

_____

_____

PRINCIPLE 4

Trust in His Promises and Vision for the Future

The righteous will live by their faithfulness to God.
—Habakkuk 2:4 (NLT)

The Lord and the Word are everlasting. When we trust in God's promises and His vision for the future, we are exercising faith that He will continue this work in us, as well. "Being confident of this, that He who began a good work in you will carry to completion until the day of Christ Jesus" (Philippians 1:6 NIV). He promises to never stop loving us. An evidence of this love is the salvation he gives us—it bears forever. God proved this through Jesus's death, forever guaranteeing our forgiveness, and by giving us the Holy Spirit as our guide to living a godly life. He gives us the Holy Spirit as proof that we belong to God. Through these actions, we can know that our sins are forgiven and that our salvation will never end.

Righteousness of God

I once read about a young boy who was on board a ship that was being tossed mercilessly on the waves. Not a sailor or passenger on board could hide his fear, except for this boy, who appeared quite calm. Asked how he could be unafraid at such a time, he replied simply, "My father is the captain. He knows how to manage this ship." We, too, must likewise trust our captain. I recently watched another David Blaine special on television and was amazed. Wait, what the. Optical illusions are reminders that things aren't always what they seem. What is seen often depends on who is doing the looking. I may not see what you see, and God sees things neither of us may see. While we tend to tolerate or overlook sin, God hates the sight of it. He is able to see into our hearts and determine what is there.

The scriptures show us what God hates. God is righteous; consequently, he hates sin. He hates all kinds of wickedness. The thing God hates the most is idolatry, which means anything or anyone we love more than Him. God also hates injustice and partiality, which means treating people differently because of race, status, and the like. "The Lord doesn't see things the way you see them. People judge by outward appearance, but the Lord looks at the heart" (1 Samuel 16:7 NLT). The law of God as revealed in Moses and recorded in the first five books of the Hebrew scriptures (Torah) speaks to those who are under the law. It's through the works of the law that the world becomes accountable to God, and through the law comes the knowledge of sin. Whenever we read, study, memorize, or meditate on the Word of God, our desire should be to know Him better. "All Scripture is God-breathed and is useful for teaching, rebuking, correcting, and training in righteousness so that the man of God may be thoroughly equipped for every good work" (2 Timothy 3:16 NIV).

Consequence of Sin

How did things get so messed up in this world? When did sin become such an issue? To understand the origin of sin, we need to go back to Genesis 3. We are introduced to Adam and Eve. They lived in the Garden of Eden, and each sinned against God. They acknowledged their sin of eating the forbidden fruit by pointing blame at the crafty serpent, each other, and God Himself for their iniquities. For consequence of their rebellious independence, He threw them out of the garden. God loved His creation but hated sin. That's important for us to remember: God hates sin, not the sinner. Because of sin's impact on humanity, we all entered this world spiritually dead, separated from God, and unable to either comprehend or understand spiritual truths. Man is blind and deaf to the message of salvation. This turning to self instead of God has infected every human since the Fall.

All of creation became contaminated with sin, and we face the penalty of sin. Sin always results in death—separation from God, from others, and from physical life. Death is the final result and ultimate price of sin. All of creation is suffering in anticipation of the return of Jesus Christ.

> For the creation was subjected to frustration, not by its own choice, but by the will of the one who subjected it, in hope that creation itself will be liberated from its bondage to decay and brought into the freedom and glory of the children of God. The difficult times of pain throughout the world are simply birth pangs. But it's not only around us— it's *within* us. (Romans 8:20–22 NIV)

We live in a spiritual war zone. Christians are forced into spiritual battle throughout their lives because of sin.

Proverbs 6:16–19 reveals six things God hates and one more that he loathes with a passion: (1) pride, eyes that are arrogant (overestimating himself or herself and underestimating others); (2) a lying tongue (deceit); (3) killing of the innocent; (4) evil scheming (a heart devising wicked thoughts and plans); (5) people who are eager to do wrong (feet that are swift to run to evil); (6) a mouth that lies under oath (false witness); (7) people who stir up dissension in the community (a troublemaker in the family). Jesus explained, "Are you still lacking in understanding also? Do you not understand that everything that goes into the mouth passes into the stomach, and is eliminated? But the things that proceed out of the mouth come from the heart, and those defile the man. For out of the man come evil thoughts, murders, adulteries, fornications, thefts, false witness, slanders. These are the things that defile" (Matthew 15:16–20 NASB).

The apostle Paul tells us, "For the wages of sin is death, but the free gift of God is eternal life in Christ Jesus our Lord" (Romans 6:23 NASB). The gospel of Jesus Christ is the only way out of this sinful condition. The good news is, Jesus broke the power of death and was resurrected to offer us new life. Everyone is equally in darkness and guilty before God. We are perfectly broken in this world with no means whatsoever to reconcile a relationship with God from our side. The world does not refer to the landmass represented by the globe of the earth. It refers to people, perspectives, and practices. John 3:16 is probably the most famous verse in the Bible, "For God so loved the world," meaning God loves all people. When my wife and I teach Sunday school, we take turns going full circle with the kids to say the memory verse with their name in replacement of "the world" and allowing the verse to speak personally to each of them. "For God so loved [your name] that He gave His one and only Son, that whoever believes in Him shall not perish but have eternal life." The kids love it. The important thing to remember is that the people God loves, and the perspectives and practices He hates are under His control.

Whatever our past may be, we have all fallen short of God's glory. Our condition is spiritually dead and charged justly that both Jews and Greeks are under sin; as it is written, "There is none righteous, not even one; there is none who understands, there is none who seeks for God; all have turned aside, together they have become useless; there is none who does good, there is not even one" (Romans 3:10–12 NASB). This truth puts all humanity in a worrisome predicament. Like sheep, we have wandered along aimlessly and cannot find the way back on our own. We are in serious need of a Savior. The Bible teaches us not to worry because God loves us, and He can be trusted to run the universe. When we worry, we're just like a dog that gnaws and twists an old bone over and over until it's finally worn out. We consider and examine our problem from every angle but God's until we've exhausted the subject and ourselves. The good news is, God is on a relentless pursuit to seek and save the lost. God never rests until all His people are found. The Shepherd promised, "I will search for the lost and bring back the strays. I will bind up the injured and strengthen the weak, but the sleek and the strong I will destroy. I will shepherd the flock with justice" (Ezekiel 34:16 NIV).

Cornerstone

Without the life and resurrection of Jesus, Christianity itself would fall to pieces. We would all be damned to hell. Every year on Christmas Day, we celebrate the birth of our Savior. On Easter Sunday, we celebrate His resurrected life. Our future hope is set in unshakable reality. When we belong to Jesus Christ, our hope of eternal life through Him is certain. When Jesus said, "It is finished" (John 19:30 NIV), He was saying, "I have paid the debt of sin for the world." Now you don't have to pay a debt for your sins because Jesus paid it and has purchased, with His own blood, a place in heaven for you and all those who believe in Him. His written Word, the Bible, flawlessly teaches people about God and the way to follow Him. "This is the verdict: Light has come into the world, but people loved darkness instead of the light because their deeds were evil. Everyone who does evil hates the light, and will not come into the light for fear that their deeds will be exposed. But whoever lives by the truth comes into the light, so that it may be seen plainly that what they have done has been done in the sight of God" (John 3:19–21 NIV). Think about your condition before your faith in Jesus. We are all deserving of death, not forgiveness. In His mercy, God does not give us what we deserve. Living the Christian life means trusting in a God we cannot see. We walk by faith, not by sight:

> I can't impress this on you too strongly. God is looking over your shoulder. Christ himself is the Judge, with the final say on everyone, living and dead. He is about to break into the open with his rule, so proclaim the message with intensity; keep on your watch. Challenge, warn, and urge your people. Don't ever quit. Just keep it simple. You're going to find that there will be times when people will have no stomach for solid teaching, but will

fill up on spiritual junk food—catchy opinions that tickle their fancy. They'll turn their backs on truth and chaos mirages. But you keep your eye on what you're doing; accept the hard times along with the good; keep the message alive; do a thorough job as God's servant. (2 Timothy 4:1–2 MSG)

We exercise faith by having a firm foundation to stand on. The cornerstone of a building is a corner piece of a building's foundation. A foundation is the first part of a building to be positioned. This is why, in leadership, the lowest level is positional. A solid foundation provides support for everything that is built upon it. It is unshakable, immovable, permanent, and essential for everything that follows. Scripture refers to Jesus Christ as our foundation. Remember He's the captain. He is to our faith everything that a foundation is to a house. We are to exercise faith and our lives only on Him, not on our good works or on things the world values.

But mark this: There will be terrible times in the last days. People will be lovers of themselves, lovers of money, boastful, proud, abusive, disobedient to their parents, ungrateful, unholy, without love, unforgiving, slanderous, without self-control, brutal, not lovers of the good, treacherous, rash, con-

ceited, lovers of pleasure rather than lovers of
God—having a form of godliness but deny-
ing its power. Have nothing to do with them.
(2 Timothy 3:1–5 NIV)

Though life's difficulties may even shake us, we must trust
His promises and vision for the future. "Be very careful then,
how you live—not as unwise but as wise, making the most of
every opportunity because the days are evil" (Ephesians 5:15–16
NIV). Because God is faithful, He has never broken a promise.
Sound character and doctrine are essential to exercising faith.
Doctrine is what you believe about scriptural teachings, and
sound doctrine matters. Paul, in his letter to Timothy, writes,
"Watch your life and doctrine closely. Persevere in them" (1
Timothy 4:16 NIV). Our hope in Jesus Christ is what makes us
persevere, and it is through perseverance that our faith matures
and we learn more about Him. We are responsible to keep our
hearts free from anything that diminishes our devotion to God.
We must guard our minds against the influences in our society
that contaminate our thoughts and behaviors. The Bible says,
"Anyone who gets so progressive in his thinking that he walks
out on the teaching of Christ, walks out on God. But whoever
stays with the teaching, stays faithful to both the Father and
the Son" (2 John 1:9 MSG). Scripture also warns us to control
our mouths in order to avoid hurtful, careless, and deceptive
speech. "He who guards his mouth and his tongue keeps himself from calamity" (Proverbs 21:23 NIV).

Takeaway: God promises to never stop loving us. An evidence of this love is the salvation He gives us—it bears forever. What God starts He finishes.

Memory Verse: "Being confident of this, that He who began a good work in you will carry to completion until the day of Christ Jesus" (Philippians 1:6 NIV).

Question to Think About: How do you respond to God when you're in a difficult situation? What examples can you share of how God has demonstrated His good work in you?

_____

_____

_____

_____

_____

_____

_____

_____

TRUST IN HIS PROMISES AND VISION FOR THE FUTURE

He's in Control of All Things

For I am convinced that neither death, nor life, nor angels, nor principalities, nor things present, nor things to come, nor powers, nor height, nor depth, nor any other created thing, will be able to separate us from the love of God, which is in Christ Jesus our Lord.

—Romans 8:38–39 (NASB)

Unlike the boss or the president, whose term is complete, nothing will force God out of power. In fact, the Bible tells us that God will always reign, and whatever He establishes cannot be altered by anyone. When everything else seems to change so quickly, God will always be the same. He's in control of all things.

> Praise the Lord, Praise the Lord, O my soul. I will praise the Lord all my life; I will sing praise to my God as long as I live. Do

not put your trust in princes, in mortal men, who cannot save. When their spirit departs, they return to the ground; on that very day their plans come to nothing. Blessed is he whose help is the God of Jacob, whose hope is in the Lord his God, the maker of heaven and earth, the sea, and everything in them—the Lord, who remains faithful forever. (Psalm 146:1–6 NIV)

Salvation is all His doing. "For by grace you have been saved through faith. And this is not your own doing: it is the gift of God, not a result of works, so that no one may boast" (Ephesians 2:8–9 ESV). We did nothing to deserve it. "He makes both us and you stand firm because we belong to Christ. He anointed us. He put His spirit in our hearts and marked us as His own. We can now be sure He will give us everything He promised us" (2 Corinthians 1:21–22 NIRV).

Understanding who God is teaches us to follow His ways, not the world's ways or the way of our own choosing. God's ways are different from our ways, and we need to learn and obey His instruction. Jesus said, "Enter through the narrow gate. For wide is the gate and broad the road that leads to destruction, and many enter through it. But small is the gate and narrow the road that leads to life, and only a few find it" (Matthew 7:13 NIV). We do not find the right road by accident. God is in control. Even when things look like they're out of control. God is still in control. We must make conscious choices each day to follow God's ways. Otherwise, the web we weave will lead to more confusion. The Bible encourages us in this: "It's in Christ that we find out who we are and what we are living for. Long before we first heard of Christ and got our hopes up, he had his eye on us, had designs on us for glorious living, part of the overall purpose he is working out in everything and everyone" (Ephesians 1:11–12 MSG). There is no way of escape. We must surrender our lives to God. King David taught us how in Psalm 139:23–24 (NLT): "Search me, O God, and know my heart; test me and know my anxious thoughts. Point out anything in me that offends You, and lead me along the path of everlasting life."

God's Faithfulness

When we are exercising faith, we are dependent on Him holding on to us, not us holding on to Him. If faith were based on us holding on to Him, we would fail Him almost immediately. Let's suppose faith was based on your ability to extend your arms out in a ninety-degree angle then down to your side while holding a three-pound dumbbell in each hand. How many times do you think you'd be able to lift it up and down? If it were up to me, I'd probably drop and fail the exercise after about twenty times. Stop trying to hold on to God. God is faithful even when we are not. The Bible says, "This is love: not that we loved God, but that He loved us and sent His Son as an atoning sacrifice for our sins" (1 John 4:10 NIV). This should bring great comfort to your spirit. Our faith rests in Him, knowing He's in control of all things. Jesus tells us, "I give them eternal life, and they shall never perish; no one can snatch them out of my hand" (John 10:28 NIV).

Jesus, the Way to the Father

One of the great tragedies of our generation is the number of children who don't know their fathers. But those who do know their fathers know that their fathers have character flaws. Apart from their earthly one, Christians, however, have a Father who is flawless. God is the Father to all who surrender their lives to Him. Our relationship to Him is an adoption; we are permanently transplanted into His family. He promises us every spiritual blessing—something of much more value to our lives than any kind of earthly possessions. As children of God, we can expect to be disciplined if we stumble or make a mistake. And we shouldn't be discouraged when this happens, because discipline shows us that God loves us. Just as good parents teach their children not to do things that will hurt them, so does our Father in heaven teach us what is best for us.

He perfectly cares for us, giving us all we need, although we may not agree with Him on what those needs are. The Father is refining His people to become more and more like His son, Jesus Christ. Jesus comforts His disciples: "My Father's house has many rooms; if that were not so, would I have told you that

I am going there to prepare a place for you? And if I go and prepare a place for you, I will come back and take you to be with me that you also may be where I am" (John 14:2–3 NIV). In the Gospel of John, Thomas said to Him, "Lord, we don't know where you are going, so how can we know the way?" Jesus answered, "I am the way and the truth and the life. No one comes to the Father except through Me. If you really know Me, you will know my Father as well. From now on, you do know Him and have seen Him" (John 14:5–7 NIV).

Eternal Life, Heaven, and Hell

Is there a difference between heaven and eternal life? Heaven and eternal life are two separate things. Eternal life is something we can receive now while we're still here on this earth. Jesus lifted up His eyes to heaven and said, "This is eternal life, that they may know You, the only true God, and Jesus Christ whom You have sent" (John 17:3 NASB). God made Himself available to us through His son, Jesus Christ. The calling of every Christian is to know Him. The Bible tells us, "And we know that the Son of God has come and has given us understanding so that we may know Him who is true; and we are in Him who is true, in His Son Jesus Christ. This is the true God and eternal life" (1 John 5:20 NASB).

Heaven is a place where Jesus is. And wherever Jesus is, there Heaven is also. So in actuality, over 2,021 years ago, heaven came down to us. Religion is bent on figuring out a way to get to heaven. Natural man tries to justify his sin; therefore, he has a deflated view of God and an inflated view of self. God didn't travel all this way to suffer and die on a cross to bring us religion. God came to reconcile our broken relationship and take us home into a relationship with God. The Bible says, "All who believe in the Son of God know in their hearts that this testimony is true. Those who don't believe this are actually calling God a liar because they don't believe what God testified about His Son. And this is what God has testified: He has given us eternal life, and this life is in His Son. Whoever has the Son has life; whoever does not have God's Son does not have life" (1 John 5:10–11 NLT).

Paul's message to the churches scattered throughout the region of Galatia taught this: "For you are all children of God through faith in Christ Jesus" (Galatians 3:26 NLT). "For through the law I died to the law so that I might live for God. I have been crucified with Christ and I no longer live, but Christ lives in me. The life I live in the body, I live by faith in the Son of God, who loved me and gave himself for me" (Galatians 2:19–20 NIV). Men cannot save themselves! The Bible points out that we all fall short of God's holy standard. Evangelist Ray Comfort, founder of the Way of the Master, uses effective techniques that pull at people's heartstrings by asking a few indisputable questions. Let's just suppose you consider yourself to be a good person. Have you ever told a lie? Ever stolen something? Ever used God's name in vain? If yes, by your own omission, you're a lying, thieving, blasphemer at heart. Now that's only three of the Ten

Commandments. The Bible says, "If you've broken just one of the ten commandments, it's like you've broken them all." If God judges you based on the Ten Commandments alone, would you consider yourself to be innocent or guilty? Heaven or hell?

Partners in Ministry explains the significance of the cross this way: Let's suppose you sin only three times a day—once verbally by saying a wrong word, once mentally by thinking a wrong thought, and once physically by committing a wrong deed. Just three sins a day would be over a thousand sins a year. That would be over seventy thousand sins in an average lifetime. What if you were to stand before a judge in a court of law in your city with seventy thousand crimes on your record? Would you expect that judge to let you go free or sentence you behind bars? Would you expect the judge to be just and do what is right? Of course, you would! You must not expect any less from God. The Bible says, "Shall not the Judge of all the earth deal justly?" God, the Judge of all the earth, is right 100 percent of the time. "I can do nothing on My own. I judge as God tells Me. Therefore, My judgement is just, because I carry out the will of the One who sent Me, not My own will" (John 5:30 NLT).

We are all guilty before God. The Bible says, "Indeed, there is not a righteous man on earth who continually does good and who never sins" (Ecclesiastes 7:20 NASB). God's written word further states, "They have all turned aside, together they have become corrupt; There is no one who does good, not even one" (Psalm 14:3 NASB). No one has ever reached heaven based on their ability or morality in this life. It is clear from Scripture that, because of your sin, you cannot make it to heaven on the basis of your good works.

The Bible clearly tells us, "The wages of sin is death." This death is eternal separation from God in a place the Bible calls hell. The Bible describes hell as a place of eternal torment and fire, "where *their worm does not die, and the fire is not quenched*" (Mark 9:44 NASB). Those who reject Christ are condemned to eternal death in hell, but for all those God came to save (sinners), they are given eternal life with Him in heaven. This is not a choice of free will. This is not a choice based on human decision either. We tend to think that God gave us some sort of ability to either accept him or not. We are conditioned to believe that nothing in life is free; we must earn it! So when we think of spiritual things, we apply this same logic.

This is a doctrinal truth: Jesus said, "You did not choose Me, but I chose you" (John 15:16 NASB). Eternal life is a free gift and given to those by whom God chooses at a perfect point in time, between birth and death. John Piper simplifies this biblical truth in that "God chose to save certain individuals. That choice was based on nothing within these people but rested solely on God's good pleasure. God is sovereign in salvation which means He is above or superior to all others; supreme in power and rank; independent of all others. He would do as He pleased. He needed no one's permission. He was under no obligation to save anyone. He would be perfectly just in choosing any of the 3 options. He could choose to save some without obligation to save others." Because salvation is a gift; it means

God gets all the credit. We did nothing to earn it. The Bible says, "For all have sinned and fall short of the glory of God" (Romans 3:23 NIV).

Mercy and Truth

What if I still consider myself to be a good person? The Bible says, "There is no one righteous, not even one; there is no one who understands; there is no one who seeks God. All have turned away, they have together become worthless; there is no one who does good, not even one" (Romans 3:11–12 NIV). We all deserve death. The Bible tells us, "By nature we are children of wrath" (Ephesians 2:3 NASB). "But God, being rich in mercy, because of His great love with which He loved us, even when we were dead in our transgressions, made us alive together with Christ" (Ephesians 2:4–5 NASB). Salvation is all His doing. "For it is by grace you have been saved, through faith—and this is not from yourselves, it is the gift of God—not by works, so that no one can boast" (Ephesians 2:8–9 NIV).

Satan (enemy) is the true destroyer of humankind, but God will one day bring peace to the earth, and violence will never again destroy His creation. How did Jesus defeat the enemy? First, He fully submitted to God and His will for His life. And second, He fully trusted the Word of God. The spiritual weapons Jesus used were the Word of God and worship. We must follow the example of how Jesus gained the victory over the enemy in the wilderness. The enemy is dumbfounded when we can praise and worship God in the midst of trial, suffering, and difficulty. We must be reminded to renew our minds and our hearts with God's Word that we may be able to stand firm against the schemes of the enemy. When we maintain our peace, we honor God, and this overwhelms the enemy, and he flees from us. The Bible says, "Therefore submit to God. Resist the devil and he will flee from you" (James 4:7 NKJV). The only way to resist the devil is with the humble truth of God's Word. No more listening to the enemy's lies; follow the teaching of Jesus. "If you hold to my teaching, you are really my disciples. Then you will know the truth, and the truth will set you free" (John 8:31–32 NIV).

The enemy is powerless now that Jesus defeated sin and death. The Bible says, "Do not be afraid, I am the first and the last, and the living One; and I was dead, and behold, I am alive forevermore, and I have the keys of death and of Hades" (Revelation 1:18 NASB). The enemy's tactics were to tempt us to doubt God and to serve him (and ourselves). The devil's lies will show us all kinds of things that will appear to be good, attractive, successful, and wonderful. A mere deception of the truth. Your life is a serious game to the enemy who operates in darkness. From the beginning, God said, "Let there be light; and there was light. God saw that the light was good; and God separated the light from the darkness" (Genesis 1:3–4 NASB). The Bible says, "The thief comes only to steal and kill and destroy; I came that they may have life and have it abundantly" (John 10:10 NASB). The enemy's goal for your life is to steal your hopes and dreams, rob you of your innocence, keep you in darkness, kill off spiritual thoughts of truth, and destroy your life and any meaningful relationships. He wants you to remain in your sins. But God had an idea, a master plan, and it was fulfilled on the cross at Calvary through His son, Jesus. The apostle Paul tells us, "There is salvation in no one else! God has given no other name under heaven by which we must be saved" (Acts 4:12 NLT). Jesus Christ is God in the flesh. The translation of Jesus's name means "God rescues." Jesus paid the penalty for all sin on the cross. Death could not hold Him, meaning that everyone who turns away from sin and puts their faith and trust in Christ will be freed from the punishment of God's wrath and have eternal life.

Worship and Wisdom

In the midst of disaster, Habakkuk chose to praise God and acknowledge that God was in control. During those tough times, it's difficult to be in the least joyful. Habakkuk has a change of heart and recommits himself to God, to His vision, and to the destiny of his nation. Regardless of what happened, he would trust the process in which God had placed him. He didn't single out praise and worship as if they were some quick prescription for the depression. Consider a prayer of the prophet Habakkuk:

> Though the cherry trees don't blossom
> and the strawberries don't ripen,
> Though the apples are worm-eaten
> and the wheat fields stunted,

Though the sheep pens are sheepless
and the cattle barns empty,
I'm singing joyful praise to God.
I'm turning cartwheels of joy to my Savior God.
Counting on God's Rule to prevail,
I take heart and gain strength.
I run like a deer.
I feel like I'm king of the mountain!
—Habakkuk 3:18–19 MSG

True worship isn't simply singing happy songs when we feel happy. It's choosing to trust God and declare that His character is perfect even when we don't understand and our hearts are breaking. Proverbs 3:5–6 NIV says, "Trust in the Lord with all your heart and lean not on your own understanding; in all your ways submit to Him, and He will make your paths straight." True victory comes when we focus on Jesus in spite of our pain or our questions.

How often do you find yourself in a dilemma over what to do in a specific situation? Remember this: to know God, this is your calling. Eternal life is the life you were called to. To glorify God, this is your purpose. We make God known by proclaiming the truth of the Gospel. Exercising faith is the responsibility of living this truth out, but in order to effectively do so, this requires godly wisdom. Godly wisdom is the ability to reach sound decisions through knowledge, insight, judgment, and discernment. In the book of James, we learn, "If any of you lacks wisdom, you should ask God, who gives generously to all without finding fault, and it will be given to you" (James 1:5 NIV). So being wise is much more than just being smart. You can rank highest in your class, but without wisdom, you will do foolish things. Getting old doesn't necessarily mean getting wise. The wise person makes choices that are rooted in the fear of God, which is the desire to please God and obey His commands. God has given us His Word, His Spirit, and one another to keep us on the right track. Godly wisdom comes as we live and walk by the Spirit. "The fruit of the Spirit is love, joy, peace, patience, kindness, goodness, faithfulness, gentleness, self-control; against such things there is no law" (Galatians 5:22 NASB). When you live by the spirit, you are exercising faith by refusing to gratify your sinful desires. Worldly wisdom runs contrary to the Spirit, which are the following: "sexual immorality, impurity, lustful pleasures, idolatry, sorcery, hostility, quarreling, jealousy, outbursts of anger, selfish ambition, dissension, division, envy, drunkenness, wild parties, and other sins like these. Those who live like this will not inherit the kingdom of God" (Galatians 5:19–21 NLT).

Redemptive Plan

The writers of the gospels are Matthew, Mark, Luke, and John. These four men lived and walked with Jesus. There are four different perspectives and viewpoints of Jesus's work on earth. Matthew wrote to the Hebrews and showed Jesus to be the king. Mark wrote to the Romans and showed Jesus to be a servant (much of Mark's Gospel is filled with information given to him from Peter). Luke wrote to the Greeks and showed Jesus to be a perfect man. And John wrote to the entire world and showed Jesus to be Mighty God. Among the four Gospels, John's unique. He gives no birth story, no account of Jesus's temptations, and none of Jesus's parables. John mostly tells about episodes from the life of Jesus not covered by the other three Gospels. Over and over, he claims that Jesus is the source of eternal life. He is the light that shines in the darkness, the Savior of the world. He is the son of God, equal with God himself. Toward the end of the book, John plainly states his purpose for writing: "that you may believe that Jesus is the Christ, the Son of God, and that by believing you may have life in His name" (John 20:31 NASB).

John compares the crucifixion of Jesus to the Old Testament account of the bronze snake (Numbers 21:8–9 NIV). The people of Israel grew impatient in the wilderness and spoke against the Lord and Moses. "Why have you brought us up out of Egypt to die in the desert? There is no bread! There is no water! And we detest this miserable food!" Then the Lord sent venomous snakes among them; they bit the people, and many Israelites died. The Lord instructed Moses, "Make a snake and put it up on a pole—anyone who is bitten can look at it and live." So Moses made a bronze snake and put it up on a pole. When the Israelites sinned, they looked at the bronze snake and were healed and saved. Jesus used the snake as a metaphor of His redemptive work. Jesus made use of the bronze snake according to its original purpose of forgiveness and restoration. This is the heart of God's redemptive plan for all aspects of life. When sin is dealt with, God's original purposes can be restored. The "good news" is, Jesus saves those who look to Him for cleansing of sin. We do not need to be perfect before we go to God. We must be in agreement with God about our sin and turn away toward Him for salvation. True repentance means letting the forgiveness you've experienced change your life.

Rejoice in the Lord

God told Habakkuk He was going to bring a conqueror, the Babylonians, to punish the wicked. This wasn't what Habakkuk wanted to hear. The Babylonians were even worse than the oppressive Israelites! When God assured Habakkuk that the Babylonians, too, would be punished, the prophet responded in Habakkuk 3:1–19 with a psalm of prayer and praise that celebrated God's power and expressed delight in God's faithfulness.

> I have heard all about you, Lord. I am filled with awe by your amazing works. In this time of our deep need, help us again as you did in years gone by. And in your anger, remember your mercy (Habakkuk 3:2 NLT).

"Rejoice in the Lord always. I will say it again: Rejoice!" (Philippians 4:4 NIV). God promised that one day He will punish all evil. We, too, can rejoice in our conqueror, Jesus Christ, for saving us from the wrath to come. The truth is, Jesus came and defeated sin once and for all by sacrificing Himself and rising from the dead three days later. Jesus paid the penalty for all sin on the cross.

Jesus' resurrection proved that God was satisfied with Jesus' blood sacrifice for sins and that God's new covenant had begun. In 1 Corinthians 15:17, Paul addressed how the resurrection is essential to the gospel. Paul writes, "And if Christ has not been raised, your faith is worthless; you are still in your sins." If Christ had remained dead, His death would have meant nothing more than yours or mine. Mankind would still be without hope in a broken world. Jesus' resurrection gives us hope that we one day too will be raised and changed. God gives us victory over death through Jesus. Let us rejoice and celebrate. Jesus is alive!

Consider Isaiah, in Isaiah 53:5–6. "He was pierced for our transgressions, He was crushed for our iniquities; the punishment that brought us peace was on Him, and by His wounds we are healed. We all, like sheep, have gone astray, each of us has turned to our own way; and the Lord has laid on Him the iniquity of us all."

Jesus didn't come to earth to condemn you; He came to save you. Meaning everyone who turns away from sin and puts their trust and confidence in Christ will have eternal life with Him. "Everyone who believes that Jesus is the Christ has been born of God" (1 John 5:1 NIV). There is no greater treasure on this earth than knowing you have eternal life. The Lord God Almighty is in control of all things on earth and in heaven. "Nothing impure will ever enter it, nor will anyone who does what is shameful or deceitful, but only those whose names are written in the Lamb's book of life" (Revelation 21:27 NIV). Because we belong to God, we can rejoice even during times of injustice, difficulty, and suffering—not because things work out the way we want, but because our future is in the hand of the One who loves us and takes great joy in us.

At the end of this chapter, I have provided a blank page for you to write down your personal psalm of prayer and praise. My prayer to each of you is that you'll allow God to speak to your heart and give you the strength, courage, wisdom, and knowledge to express your thoughts and questions on paper. Then lift it up in prayer to the Living God, and thank Him for insight in showing you His truth. I promise God is listening to every word.

The Bible is God's love letter to us. He wrote it for everyone. God's plan and desire was to write His law with permanent marker in the minds and hearts of His people. And that is what He does when He gives the Holy Spirit to those who believe in Jesus. God taught Habakkuk to obey whatever He commands. To write it down. Like Habakkuk, we can rejoice because God is in control. We, too, worship Him regardless of our present or past circumstances. The Bible teaches us, "The righteous will live by their faithfulness to God" (Habakkuk 2:4 NLT). Here are the five guiding principles Habakkuk preserved for us as an example so we also can exercise FAITH:

1. Follow God as the leader.
2. Always wait for His instruction.
3. Immediately listen to His voice.
4. Trust in His promises and vision for the future.
5. He's in control of all things.

What Now?

God has a plan to reach the world, and it's through you! "God chose you to be saved through the sanctifying work of the Spirit and through the belief in the truth. He called you to this through our gospel, that you might share in the glory of our Lord Jesus Christ" (2 Thessalonians 2:13–14 NIV). The gospel means "good news," and it is meant to be a blessing for all people. Jesus Christ was the ultimate servant. He put aside His position in heaven to take on human form. He healed and fed people while He was on the earth, and in the greatest act of servanthood, He gave His life for us. Jesus taught the people about God. He explained what the scriptures meant, and He taught with an incredible authority that the people had never seen or heard before. Learning and teaching are essential to our Christian faith. Believing is the first step to telling others about Jesus Christ. Let me encourage you: if you know enough to believe, you know enough to proclaim the life-changing message of Jesus Christ with others. Jesus told us to carry on His work. As the old saying goes, "Give a man a fish, and you feed him for a day, but teach a man to fish, and you feed him for a lifetime." We are to instruct people not only in the truths about salvation but also in how to obey God and apply what they hear.

We're called to serve God and others, using Jesus as our greatest example. It is now our job to bless the nations by proclaiming the good news of the death and resurrection of Jesus Christ. "Go and make disciples of all nations, baptizing them in the name of the Father, and of the Son, and of the Holy Spirit, and teaching them to obey everything I have commanded you" (Matthew 28:19–20 NIV). Put into practice these five principles of faith if you're starting a new ministry in your community, a nonprofit, a business, or training up your own household. This design is the foundation for the love life God intends men and women to experience, even in their own marriages. Marriage is a daily opportunity for a husband and a wife to demonstrate Christ's love for another person: "Wives, submit yourselves to your own husbands as you do to the Lord" (Ephesians 5:22 NIV), and "Husbands, love your wives, just as Christ loved the church and gave himself up for her" (Ephesians 5:25 NIV).

Things are changing at a rapid pace. Maybe you've been experiencing a high level of anxiety and unrest, but we don't have to be discouraged in these uncertain times. We can approach our daily concerns with confidence. God is in control of all things. God's Word never changes. The Apostle Peter wrote, "For you have been born again, but not to a life that will quickly end. Your new life will last forever because it comes from the eternal, living word of God (1 Peter 1:23 NLT). The Lord promises to be our constant guide, provider, and protector. Meditate on His promises day and night. Treasure them. Store up His word in your heart. "If God is for us, who can ever be against us?" (Romans 8:31 NLT). Failure to trust and obey expresses a disbelief in our Savior's ability to meet all our needs, and it suggests we think we can do a better than our Savior is doing for us.

Jesus promised to give us peace in the midst of suffering, injustice, and difficulty. Because God is faithful, He has never broken a promise. We can trust Him. In these troubling times, we can still have peace, for He tells us:

> Do not be anxious about anything, but in every situation, by prayer and petition, with thanksgiving, present your requests to God. And the peace of God, which transcends all understanding, will guard your hearts and your minds in Christ Jesus. (Philippians 4:6–7 NIV)

We all have reasons for not helping the needy. Many of us worry that we'll be taken advantage of by some false tale or con game. Others don't know which voice to respond to among all those crying out on the streets. Some of us are simply focused on ourselves that we can't hear. But the consequences for shutting our ears is eternal. God has given us a responsibility to the poor and needy as a part of His redemptive plan for humanity. Like the Good Samaritan, we need to keep an open heart toward those the Lord brings into our path. Everything we do should be done to glorify God—every action, every thought, and every word. Use your spiritual gift to serve the local church and bless others. Pursue faith, love, compassion, and care for others like our Savior, Jesus Christ shown us. "In the same way let your light shine before others, that they may see your good deeds and glorify your Father in heaven" (Matthew 5:16 NIV). Through Christ's strength, we have the ability to exercise the principles of faith and do remarkable things for God.

Takeaway: God is faithful even when we are not.

Memory Verse: "This is love: not that we loved God, but that He loved us and sent His Son as an atoning sacrifice for our sins" (John 4:10 NIV).

Question to Think About: How do you celebrate God's power and express delight in God's faithfulness?

_____

_____

_____

_____

_____

_____

_____

_____

_____

_____

_____

_____

_____

_____

_____

_____

_____

_____

_____

_____

_____

_____

My Personal Psalm of Faith

_____

_____

_____

_____

_____

_____

_____

_____

_____

_____

_____

Notes

Introduction

1. Exodus 20:3 NIV.
2. Swindoll, Charles.
3. Romans 12:2 MSG.
4. Deuteronomy 31:8 NLT.
5. John 16:33 NLT.
6. 1 John 5:4–5 NLT.
7. Hebrews 11:1 NIV.
8. Ephesians 2:8 NIV.
9. Philippians 1:6 NIV.
10. Romans 15:4 NLT.

Principle 1: Follow God as the Leader

1. Proverbs 3:5–6 NIV.
2. Mark 1:17 NIV.
3. Ephesians 1:11–12 MSG.
4. Jeremiah 31:3 NIV.
5. Psalm 145:17 NIV.
6. Isaiah 30:18 NIV.
7. Romans 8:5 NIV.

8. Psalm 51:4 NIV.

9. Psalm 23 NKJV.

10. Job 1:1 NIV.

11. Romans 8:1 NIV.

12. Romans 8:39 NIV.

13. Habakkuk chapter 1–3.

14. 1 Corinthians 4:20 MSG.

15. Colossians 1:26 NLT.

16. Colossians 1:15–23 NLT.

17. John 1:14 NIV.

18. Exodus 20:4 NLT.

19. Exodus 2:3 NKJV.

20. Habakkuk 1:11 NLT.

21. Habakkuk 2:18 NIV.

22. Ephesians 2:12 NLT.

23. Romans 5:8 NASB.

24. John 15:5 NLT.

25. John 14:6 NIV.

26. Ephesians 1:7 NASB.

27. John 4:14 NIV.

28. 1 Samuel 24:6 NIV.

29. John 10:11 NIV.

30. Psalm 23:6 NIV para.

31. Matthew 22:37 NIV.

32. Acts 4:12 NLT

33. Mark 1:7–8 NIV.

34. John 1:29 NIV.

35. John 1:32–34 NIV.

36. Luke 7:22 NIV.

37. John 3:36 NIV.

38. John 3:30 NKJV.

39. Matthew 6:6 NIV.

40. Psalm 23:4 NASB.

41. Psalm 23:4 NKJV.

42. Romans 8:26 NLT.

43. James 1:22 NIV.

44. Matthew 5:3 NASB.

45. Mark 10:27 NIV.

46. Psalm 51:17 NLT.

47. Matthew 22:37–40 NIV.

Principle 2: Always Wait for His Instruction

1. Psalm 5:3 NIV.

2. Exodus 16:4 NLT.

3. John 6:48 NIV.

4. Shrader, Tom.

5. Romans 5:3–5 NLT.

6. Matthew 11:28 NLT.

7. Palau, Luis.

8. Romans 5:17 NLT.

9. Genesis 3.

10. Stedman, Ray.

11. John 6:48 NASB.

12. John 6:51 NIV.

13. 2 Timothy 3:12–13 NIV.

14. Jeremiah 29:11 NIV.

15. James 1:2–3 NIV.

16. Isaiah 55:9 NASB.

17. 1 John 5:3–4 NASB.

18. Luke 11:23–28 NASB.

19. James 1:12 NIV.

20. Romans 8:28–30 NLT.

21. Romans 13:11–14 NASB.

22. Romans 3:23 NIV.

23. Romans 6:23 NASB.

Principle 3: Immediately Listen to His Voice

1. 1 John 4:19 NIV.

2. John 10:27–28 NASB.

3. Romans 10:17 NLT.

4. Ezekiel 34:11–16 MSG.

5. Matthew 7:3–5 NIV.

6. Matthew 15:16–20 NASB.

7. Hebrews 4:12 NIV.

8. Psalm 19:4 NLT.

9. Psalm 26:2 NIV.

10. John 3:8 NIV.

Principle 4: Trust in His Promises and Vision for the Future

1. Habakkuk 2:4 NLT.
2. Philippians 1:6 NIV.
3. 1 Samuel 16:7 NLT.
4. 2 Corinthians 1:21–22 ESV.
5. 2 Timothy 3:16 NIV.
6. Romans 8:20–22 NIV.
7. Proverbs 6:16–19 NIV.
8. Matthew 15:16–20. NASB.
9. Romans 6:23 NASB.
10. Romans 3:10–12 NASB.
11. Ezekiel 34:16 NIV.
12. John 19:30 NIV.
13. John 3:19–21 NIV.
14. Psalm 107:1 NKJV.
15. 2 Timothy 4:1–2 MSG.
16. 2 Timothy 3:1–5 NIV.
17. Ephesians 5:15–16 NIV.
18. 1 Timothy 4:16 NIV.
19. 2 John 1:9 MSG.
20. Proverbs 21:23 NIV.

Principle 5: He's in Control of All Things

1. Romans 8:38–39 NASB.
2. Psalm 146:1–6 NIV.
3. Ephesians 2:8–9 ESV.

4. Matthew 7:13 NIV.

5. Ephesians 1:11–12 MSG.

6. Psalm 139:23–24 NLT.

7. 1 John 4:10 NIV.

8. John 10:28 NIV.

9. John 14:2–3 NIV.

10. John 14:5–7 NIV.

11. John 17:3 NASB.

12. John 1 John 5:20 NASB.

13. 1 John 5:10–11 NLT.

14. Galatians 3:26 NLT.

15. Galatians 2:19–20 NIV.

16. Comfort, Ray.

17. John 5:30 NLT.

18. Ecclesiastes 7:20 NASB.

19. Psalm 14:3 NASB.

20. Mark 9:44 NASB.

21. John 15:16 NASB.

22. Piper, John.

23. Romans 3:23 NIV.

24. Romans 3:11–12 NIV.

25. Ephesians 2:3 NASB.

26. Ephesians 2:4–5 NIV.

27. Ephesians 2:8–9 NIV.

28. James 4:7 NKJV.

29. John 8:31–32 NIV.

30. Revelation 1:18 NASB.

31. Genesis 1:3–4 NASB.

32. John 10:10 NASB.

33. Acts 4:12 NLT.

34. Habakkuk 3:18–19 MSG.

35. James 1:5 NIV.

36. Galatians 5:22–23 NASB.

37. Galatians 5:19–21 NLT.

38. John 20:31 NASB.

39. Numbers 21:8–9 NIV.

40. Habakkuk 3:1–19 NIV.

41. Habakkuk 3:2 NLT.

42. Philippians 4:4 NIV.

43. 1 Corinthians 15:17 NASB.

44. Isaiah 53:5–6 NIV.

45. 1 John 5:1 NIV.

46. Hebrews 12:2 NIV.

47. Revelation 21:27 NIV.

48. Habakkuk 2:4 NLT.

49. 2 Thessalonians 2:13–14 NIV.

50. Matthew 28:19–20 NIV.

51. Ephesians 5:25 NIV.

52. 1 Peter 1:23 NLT.

53. Romans 8:31 NLT.

54. Philippians 4:6–7 NIV.

55. Matthew 5:16 NIV

About the Author

 Joe B. Lamphere was inspired to author his first book, *Hope in a Broken World,* encouraging us in times of uncertainty and challenging us to keep our hearts and minds focused on things above—right in the midst of affliction. Born on May 15, 1971, Joe was the youngest of seven children and was raised in the northwest suburbs of Chicago, Illinois. Joe began a successful sales executive career in the highly competitive international logistics industry. That career was interrupted in the fall of 2003, when God extended His saving grace and mercy to Joe and led him in a completely different direction. Since then, Joe received a bachelor's degree in 2007 and his master's degree in 2009 from the University of Phoenix. Joe has been involved in the study of God's Word, teaching the Word of God in Sunday-school ministry, serving in different age groups over the past 17 years at Redemption Church. Joe has a great level of enthusiasm as he teaches the children and has a wonderful way of communicating and reflecting the love of Christ through the Bible lessons, worship and activities. Joe and his lovely wife, Laura, celebrated their twenty-fifth wedding anniversary in 2020 and are parents of three young adult children. They make their home in Mesa, Arizona.